NORTHR

IN CONVERSATION

NORTHROP FRYE
IN CONVERSATION

DAVID CAYLEY

Copyright © 1992 by David Cayley

First published in 1992 by
House of Anansi Press Limited
1800 Steeles Avenue West
Concord, Ontario
L4K 2P3

CBC logo used by permission

Canadian Cataloguing in Publication Data

Frye, Northrop, 1912-1991

Northrop Frye in conversation

ISBN 0-88784-525-8

1. Frye, Northrop, 1912-1991 — Interviews.
I. Cayley, David.   II. Title.

PN75.F7A3 1992   801'.95'092   C92-093284-3

Cover design: Brant Cowie/ArtPlus Limited
Typesetting: Tony Gordon Ltd.
Printed and bound in Canada

House of Anansi Press gratefully acknowledges the support of
the Canada Council, Ontario Arts Council and Ontario
Publishing Centre in the development of writing and
publishing in Canada.

Contents

PREFACE

I first met Northrop Frye in 1984 when I interviewed him for a program called "History and the New Age," which I was preparing for CBC Radio's *Ideas* series where I work. Peter Gzowski once described Frye as an interviewer's nightmare: a man who actually answered the questions he was asked rather than embellishing them. His answers were usually short, sometimes cryptic, occasionally gruff, and they often ended in conversation-stopping aphorisms. On this first occasion I chattered nervously while I set up my tape recorder. Frye's seraphic smile and patient, unyielding demeanor did little to put me at ease. I then stammered my way through an hour-long interview in which Frye gave brief, pointed answers to my long and sometimes pointless questions.

I returned twice in the succeeding years — Frye was always gracious about receiving interviewers, despite his evident lack of relish for the procedure — once to talk about Canadian culture and once to talk about Blake. In both cases the rhythm of the conversation remained fairly jerky. This made me reluctant to undertake the project my colleagues kept urging on me: a series devoted to the ideas of Frye himself. However, in 1989, through the good offices of Frye's secretary Jane Widdicombe and Sara Wolch, my colleague and producer and a friend of Frye's, it was finally all arranged. For a week in December, Frye and I spent each morning in recorded conversation. Sara and I and our recording engineer, Brian Hill, turned up at Frye's Massey College office every morning at nine and by midweek had begun to feel quite at home there. Sara's presence helped to create a more relaxed atmosphere, and the fact that I had spent the previous months steeping myself in Frye's work helped me to dig beneath the surface of the epigrammatic answers Frye sometimes gave to questions he had been asked once too often. Whatever the reason, the interview possessed a fullness and flow that I had not previously experienced with Frye, and we ended our conversation on Friday in peaceful silence, gazing out through gently falling snow into the quiet courtyard of the college. Just over a year later Northrop Frye died.

After the *Ideas* series on Frye had received its first broadcast in February of 1970, I sent the unedited tapes of the interview to Robert Denham at Roanoke College, in Salem, Virginia. Denham has written both a critical study called *Northrop Frye and Critical Method* and an annotated bibliography of primary and secondary sources on Frye's work. He is also the editor of the *Northrop Frye Newsletter*, which he uses to update his bibliography and publish current writing by or about Frye. I thought he might want to publish excerpts from the interview in the newsletter. A few months later I received a bound and virtually camera-ready transcription of the entire interview and a call from Denham asking my permission to have it published. I agreed, and then later learned that House of Anansi, already the publisher of CBC Radio's annual Massey Lectures, was interested in the manuscript. Bob Denham, and Peter Blaney of the McGill University Press, who were then considering it for publication, graciously consented to return it to me. The present volume is the result. I thank Bob Denham for all the work he did on the manuscript and for his having envisioned this book in the first place. And I thank Sara Wolch for all she did to arrange the interview and make it a success.

I have begun with an introductory essay in which I offer an appreciation of Frye's life and work. This is intended to give context to the interview that follows, since my approach to Frye was obviously shaped by my understanding of his work. The interview has been lightly edited, first by Bob Denham, then by me to eliminate clumsiness and occasionally to clarify my questions. (Frye, obviously, did not have this luxury, but neither did he need it.) I have also added some material from my earlier interviews with Frye, where I thought it added something to this conversation, and joined segments of the interview that occurred on different days but seemed to belong together in the interests of narrative coherence or thematic unity. Other than that, what you will read here is what happened in those five days.

Northrop Frye once remarked to his biographer John Ayre that his work was really his biography. Ayre says that he at first discounted this observation but later came to see that it was true.[1] Frye has expressed himself with remarkable completeness in his more than twenty books; and even the wit, variety, and originality of his formulations cannot entirely disguise the fact that, like most of us, he is often saying the same thing. This book, then, can hardly claim to add anything to the Frye corpus. But it does present Frye in conversation rather than *ex cathedra*, and it does offer the reader a summary of Frye's main ideas in a compact and accessible form. I hope that for those already familiar with Frye it will offer at least the pleasure of hearing his voice again, and that for those for whom it is an introduction it will be the beginning of a great intellectual adventure.

DAVID CAYLEY
Toronto

INTRODUCTION

The procession entered Convocation Hall in full academic panoply and followed the lieutenant-governor of Ontario and the great mace of the University of Toronto toward the podium. The majesty of the organ and the brilliant colors of the hooded gowns might have been nothing more than an ironic evocation of faded glories had it not been for the occasion: a gathering of friends, students, readers, and colleagues to honor the passing six days before of Northrop Frye. Frye had often spoken of how he tried to teach from within the personality of Milton or Blake or whomever he was teaching. As his memorial service proceeded, I felt that all of us gathered there were within Frye's personality, and it was this personality that lent grandeur and dignity to

what might otherwise have seemed merely pomp-
ous. This effect intensified as some thirteen colleagues and former students rose to remember their
friend and mentor. Listening to how they spoke of
him, I realized that Frye had actually embodied the
ideal university, which he called "the engine-room
of society,"[2] and had brought this vision alive for
others. He did not evoke a glorious past or a more
glorious future. He pointed to what was possible in
the plain circumstances of the present; and, through
the force, serenity, and commitment of his personality, he made it possible.

In his books Frye had sometimes pointed to the
giant forms within which writers have embodied
their intuition that human life has a more coherent
and comprehensive shape than is perceptible to
common sense. "A Commonwealth should be but
one giant Christian personage," says Milton.[3] "Spirits," according to Blake, "are organized men."[4]
Rilke, in the *Duino Elegies*, imagines a blind angel
containing all time and space looking within himself.[5] Proust speaks of men as "giants immersed in
time."[6] Sitting in Convocation Hall on January 29,
1991, I began to imagine Northrop Frye's life and
work as one of these more inclusive forms that
draw reality into order, meaning, and direction,
and all of us present as comprehended within this
form.

Northrop Frye had arrived at the University of
Toronto sixty-two years before as a young Maritimer
of modest means whose cloth cap contrasted with
the more sophisticated hats of his Ontario class-
mates. His biographer John Ayre relates an early

encounter with a wealthy fellow freshman who, on their introduction, presented Frye with a visiting card. Frye, only temporarily nonplussed, responded with a complimentary ticket to an international typing contest to which his prowess as a secretary in Moncton had won him an invitation.[7]

Like his fellow students at Victoria College, Frye's background was Methodist. His grandfather had been a circuit-riding preacher, and by this time Frye himself had enrolled as a candidate for the United Church ministry. It was a heritage he would transform but never forsake. The Methodism from which he came was both radical and authoritarian. It was radical in drawing inspiration directly from the Bible without priestly, liturgical, or doctrinal intermediations, and radical, as well, in its opposition to church establishments. Yet it was also characterized by a rigid and repressive morality whose origins can be seen in this child-rearing advice Susanna Wesley wrote to her son John, the church's founder: "I insist on conquering the wills of children . . . Whatever pain it cost, conquer their stubbornness . . . Let a child from a year old have nothing he cries for; absolutely nothing, great or small . . . Let him do as he is bid, if you would whip him ten times running to effect it. Let none persuade you it is cruelty to do this; it is cruelty not to do it."[8]

Frye shucked off this repressive morality at a young age. Years later he told an interviewer that he "remembered walking along St. George Street to high school and just suddenly that whole shitty and smelly garment [of fundamentalist teaching I had all my life] just dropped off into the sewers and stayed there. It was like the Bunyan feeling, about the burden of sin falling off his back, only with me it was a burden of anxiety."[9]

He commented further on this crucial experience in a letter to his friend Roy Daniells. "In early adolescence I suddenly realized, with an utter and complete conviction of which I have never lost one iota since, that the whole apparatus of afterlife in heaven and hell, unpardonable sins and the like was a lot of junk . . . I think I decided very early, without realizing it at the time, that I was going to accept out of religion only what made sense to me as a human being. I was not going to worship a God whose actions, judged by human standards, were contemptible."[10]

Frye established the standard from which he would never deviate at a remarkably young age. When he encountered the work of the English poet William Blake, he saw with the same intense clarity how he could establish this standard within his own tradition. Blake himself came from a left-wing, "inner light" Protestant tradition, and he taught that the Bible had to be read in its imaginative and not its literal sense. Through Blake, Frye saw that "the lugubrious old stinker up in the sky that I had heard so much about existed all right, but . . . his name was Satan [and] his function was to promote tyranny in society and repression in the mind."[11] This was the God Blake called old Nobodaddy, "his heavens . . . writ with curses from pole to pole."[12] Blake believed this God to be a compound of superstition and sexual repression and read the Bible as the story of the passing over of this image into the Divine Humanity of Jesus. "Man can have no idea of anything greater than man," he wrote, "as a cup cannot contain more than its capaciousness."[13] It follows that we can know God only as man. We cannot perceive God, Frye later wrote in his commentary on this passage, we can perceive only *as* God.[14] In this conception God moves from an objective reality in front of us to a position that is, in effect, behind us or within us. "Those who envy or calumniate great men, hate God," Blake says, "for there is no other God."[15] God is embodied in creative acts and can have no other existence for us. It is not that what is more than human cannot exist, but that we cannot know it. This is why Frye so often reverted to the little Latin tag that he found in Vico, *verum factum.* It means that what is true for us is what we have made, and we can't understand what we haven't made because our perceptions are inevitably constructive acts.

Frye said a number of times that he learned almost everything he knew from Blake. One tends to discount such a statement when it comes from a thinker as formidable as Frye, and, when I first heard it, I think I responded like Allan Bloom, who once said that as a student at the University of Chicago he was convinced that the professor who taught him Pericles must be greater than Pericles himself.[16] But the more I read of Frye, and the more of Blake, the more I saw that Frye's statement lacked any trace of art. Frye absorbed and transmitted Blake in a way that went far beyond what is normally meant by influence. When reviewers of *Fearful Symmetry,* Frye's book about Blake, expressed irritation that they couldn't tell where Blake left off and

Frye began, their complaints were idle but their observation accurate. When I read in Frye's posthumous *The Double Vision* that the natural man can't distinguish what he believes from what he believes he believes,[17] I know I am hearing an echo of the first text Blake ever engraved, "There Is No Natural Religion," where he says that "Reason, or the ratio of all we have already known, is not the same that it shall be when we know more."[18] And even to say "echo" implies imitation, whereas in fact Frye had long since made Blake's principles entirely his own.

Frye's encounter with Blake, along with his early and definitive rejection of the repressive side of his Methodist heritage, colored everything he would subsequently create. Freeing himself from religious anxiety, while remaining engaged with those parts of his religious heritage which made sense to him as a human being, he never got stuck in a rebellious reaction. He needed to rebel against projected ancestors and cloudy Gods as little as he needed to praise or worship them. Instead he went to work, believing, as he wrote to his future wife Helen in 1935, that "as soon as you get to work, you're being religious."[19]

The arduous, agnostic, and confidently Protestant spirit of this youthful letter remained typical. There was never anything tentative about Northrop Frye. "You only know what you're doing," he said, "when what you want to do and what you have to do are exactly the same thing."[20] Frye knew what he had to do, and this knowledge gave his thought the air of imperturbable assurance that his critics find so infuriating and his admirers so inspiriting. There was no pride in his firm and confident judgments, but no false modesty either. He knew his own mind with a clarity most of us only dream of, and he never found any reason to change it. "No man can change his principles,"[21] Blake had said, and Frye's work exhibits an astonishing consistency from the first word he wrote to the last.

Following his ordination in 1936 Frye left Canada for Merton College, Oxford, and further literary studies. He returned on the eve of war in 1939. On his homeward journey he found himself on board a ship in the foggy Gulf of St. Lawrence suddenly aware that he was surrounded by five invisible Canadian provinces. Out of this poetic insight into Canada's political geography grew a theory of Canadian culture so influential that it now seems commonplace. The generation of thought from insight rather than analysis was typical of Frye. In *The Double Vision* he remarked that he "had spent the better part of seventy years writing out the implications of insights that have taken up considerably less than an hour of all those years."[22] In this case what later flowered was a view of Canada's essential difference from the United States.

An eighteenth-century traveller approaching the United States encountered a seaboard civilization gradually unrolling westward in an orderly, if violent advance. Approaching Canada he was swallowed by the yawning mouth of the Gulf of St. Lawrence like Jonah into the belly of the whale. In the U.S. the wilderness lay beyond a distinct frontier; in Canada it surrounded the country's scattered settlements, turning them into insecure garrisons and engendering what Frye called "the garrison mentality."[23] In the U.S. the Puritan founders' providentialist myth of a chosen people and a promised land drove all before it, creating a society in which it made sense to speak of "un-American activities." In Canada, as historian Syd Wise has pointed out, chosen peoples abounded and no single unifying myth ever prevailed. The creation of an enlightened and virtually sacred Constitution introduced what Frye called "a deductive pattern" into American political life.[24] This settled pattern produced the space in which such authors as Hawthorne, Melville, Poe, and Emerson could thrive. Canada, with its harsh landscapes, conflicting polities, and threatened loyalty to an often indifferent mother country, could be governed only according to an inductive pattern of compromise and improvisation. The insecurity of its "garrisons" gave civic life a characteristic note of rhetorical belligerence that was inimical to more imaginative ways of using words. The priority of pressing questions of political identity inhibited the development of artistic cultures and kept the arts in provincial tutelage to outworn metropolitan models. Eventually, according to Frye, these provincial cultures began to pass over into more authentic regional cultures, and Canadian literature began the flowering of which Frye's own writings form so much a part.

Many of the thoughts I have just summarized were not expressed until much later, in Frye's celebrated conclusion to *The Literary History of Canada* (1965) and in the essays published in *The Bush Garden* (1974) and *Divisions on a Ground* (1982). They were certainly not all present on the deck of the ship bringing him home in 1939. And yet, like Mozart who said that he would sometimes see a composition "all at one look," much of Frye's work really did begin in such images and in his ability to read them. He worked by insight, not argument, and his essays take the form of unitary constellations of ideas, rather than analytical excursions.

Upon his return to Toronto in 1939 Frye immediately assumed a heavy teaching burden, and, as he taught, he worked his way deeper into the books he was teaching. "I . . . read with tremendous intensity, and in my earlier years particularly, every text that I read that I was going to teach, or anything that I read on the scale of say Dante or so forth, is just a mass of marginalia written in pencil. I simply could not read books that didn't have wide margins, and that was one way of soaking myself into the book so that I became a part of it and it became a part of me."[25]

The classroom also became Frye's laboratory, a place where he could try out his ideas. He decided at once that he would write out his lectures only after he had given them. This principle eventually extended to his published writings as well. Almost all of Frye's published essays, and there are some three hundred odd, began life as lectures. He wrote down only what had already been proved in oral performance, and audiences from Rome to Roanoke, Virginia, can testify to having heard *ex tempore* from Frye's lips what they later read word for word in one of his books. "What we express badly, we do not know" was one of his axioms.[26]

Frye wrote a melodious, well-balanced prose —
A. C. Hamilton in his wonderful *Northrop Frye: An
Anatomy of His Criticism* even scans a sentence and
finds it entirely metrical — but it also had a plain,
direct quality, which came from the priority of
speech in its creation. The vigor and occasional
pleasing bluntness of his expression also resulted
from a principled decision to try always to address
a general audience rather than just ruffling up his
feathers for a tiny coterie of colleagues and fellow
critics. Where Frye's books are difficult, the difficulty is inherent in the subject, not the style.

All his life Northrop Frye denounced the idea that
words merely imitate ideas that exist independently
of those words. He calls this "the fallacy of the
substantial idea," believing with Blake that "ideas
cannot be given but in their minutely appropriate
words."[27] This is why we do not know what we
express badly: the thought and its expression are one
act. Even in purely descriptive writing, which tries
to imitate precisely some object outside of us, the
words will display a will of their own, forming
self-contained grammatical fictions and drawing attention away from nature and into their own fictive
intensity.

All writing is constructive to some extent, and
artistic writing expressly so. The theories of art that
prevailed until the age of Blake and Herder held that
art was imitation, an attempt to copy what God had
already done better in creating the world. Disillu-
sioned modern writers have tried to return to this
theme. C. S. Lewis says that the imagination reflects
"heavenly truth."[28] T. S. Eliot also believes that po-

etry mirrors a higher spiritual order.[29] Frye completely rejects this idea, believing art and religion to be constructive activities within us and not attempts to point at objectively existing realities.

Since Frye insists that criticism is part of literature — critics, he says, do not judge works of art, they join with writers in judging the human condition[30] — it follows that his own writing is constructive in this sense and shares the qualities he finds in the Bible, for example, where everything is potentially identified with everything else. (There is a passage in *Science and the Modern World* where Whitehead comments that "in a sense everything is everywhere at all times." Frye read the book at college — "the first book of philosophy that I read . . . purely for pleasure" — and described this passage as his "initiation into what Christianity means by spiritual vision.")[31] A. C. Hamilton remarks of a sentence of Frye's that "if it alone of all his writing had survived, like an anthropologist shaping Neanderthal man from one bone sliver, I could reconstruct *The Anatomy [of Criticism]*."[32] In my *Ideas* profile of Northrop Frye, Hamilton elaborated this point:

> Frye has an encompassing vision . . . All of his works . . . tend to be brief *Anatomys*, and anything Frye says is not part of a logical chain but really contains everything in miniature . . . An apt analogy, and it's an appropriate one for Frye because of his background, [is the way in which] ministers or rabbis or whatever religious person of authority . . . can take one passage from the Bible . . . or

the Koran and . . . reconstruct . . . the whole basis of their religion out of it . . . It's called a pericope . . . among preachers. You can take a passage of scripture and then elaborate that into the whole of Christian belief. And Frye has a quality of centrality, of . . . comprehensiveness that allows him to say amost everything within a brief statement.[33]

Frye's style is aphoristic and intense, and a publisher may some day do well with a collection of his epigrams along the lines of Blake's "Proverbs of Hell" or the once celebrated little red book of Chairman Mao. This penetrating wit is not an adornment but the very heart of his approach. "It may be doubted," he says, "whether we ever really call an idea profound unless we are pleased by the wit of its expression."[34] Wit embodies the unity of thought and expression. With Frye it can take many forms. There is the condensed and explosive metaphysical wit of a statement like "Redemption requires a God, but a God within time is no better off than we are, and a God wholly free of time is of no use to us."[35] There is the deadpan satire of a throwaway line like this comment on the Second Law of Thermodynamics, tossed off in the middle of a discussion of tragedy: "The law of entropy applies only to closed systems, and there is no certainty that the entire universe is a closed system, or even that there is a universe, but the law sounds so pointlessly lugubrious that it instantly carried conviction to many people."[36] And then there are the pithy sayings which, as Frye said of some of Milton's memorable lines, separate from their context "and start chasing themselves around your skull": "Faith is based on fiction cause it has no facts to go on."[37] "There are no dead ideas in literature, only tired readers."[38] "There is never anything underneath a persona except another persona."[39] "A poet is a myth's way of making another myth."[40] And so on. As a writer and teacher, Frye worked by the intensification of insight, the strengthening of that power in words that can carry us beyond ourselves; and, according to his own principle of metaphorical correspondence, the style was the man.

In 1947 Frye published *Fearful Symmetry*, a 400-page study of William Blake. By then the book had been through five rewrites, the penultimate draft being half again as long as what the Princeton University Press published. By 1935, he was already writing to Helen that he had "spun [Blake] round like a teetotum. I've torn him into tiny shreds and teased and anatomized him with pincers."[41] Years later he advised aspiring critics to adopt a particular writer as "spiritual preceptor." "It seems to me," he said, "that growing up inside a mind so large that one has no sense of claustrophobia within it is an irreplaceable experience in humane studies."[42] Frye had grown up inside Blake's mind, and he was convinced that Blake's writings were the golden string that would lead him first to a new poetics, which he outlined in *The Anatomy of Criticism*, and eventually to a new understanding of religion, which he would put forward in *The Great Code* and *Words with Power*. "Read Blake or go to Hell," he wrote with youthful grandiosity in 1935, "that's my message to the modern world."[43]

To Frye, Blake was the first person who had really understood the modern situation. Science had transformed the heavens from a realm of quintessence into a vast and barren mechanism. Revolution had disenchanted political authority. Industrialization had disenchanted nature. A religious structure that patently sanctified an unjust social order and a God who was "an allegory of Kings and nothing else" would no longer do.[44] Blake, in effect, turned the world upside down and, in doing so, showed Frye the cosmological and diagrammatic dimension in the literary imagination that Frye emphasized ever afterward.

In Blake's prophetic books, the enthroned God who presides over an elaborately ranked projection of the social order becomes the wintry figure of Urizen. Urizen, as his name suggests, is a caricature of human reason, and a parody of God the Father. He is a hopeless God, trapped in his own "iron laws,"[45] a symbol of humanity's creative power alienated and imprisoned within an abstract divinity. "The primal priest," Blake calls him; and, "from the sorrows of [his] soul" stretch the twisted cords which ensnare the world in "the net of religion." Blake rejects this vacuous and tyrannical image of divinity and instead imagines the divine as working from within and below to rebuild a ruined creation. Instead of hallowing the shell of earthly existence, he wants to break it. He denounces the passive contemplation of an objective world, which he calls natural religion, in favor of the active imagination that approaches the divine "on the fiery chariot of . . . contemplative thought."[46]

The elements of Blake's Christianity are not in themselves new. Poet Kathleen Raine devoted two fat volumes called *Blake and Tradition* to revealing his many antecedents. These range from Platonism and Gnosticism to Anabaptism and the antinomianism of earlier English sects like the Ranters of the Civil War period. But Blake often took from his sources what served his art and discarded the rest, and he certainly recreates the traditions from which he draws. Blake had been known to the pre-Raphaelites, to Yeats, and even to older scholars such as Foster Damon, but Frye was the first to reveal the full cosmological sweep of Blake's prophetic genius.

To Frye, Blake summed up everything that was valuable in Romanticism, and Romanticism, Frye says, "is the first major phase in an imaginative revolution which has carried on until our own day and has by no means completed itself yet."[47] *Fearful Symmetry* demonstrated this point persuasively and made a lot of people see that a renovated Romanticism — a Romanticism "come of age,"[48] as Owen Barfield said — might be a juicier and more attractive option than either the modest empiricism of the so-called New Critics or the bitter road from pessimism to reaction that Eliot had taken. The book began an extended vogue for Romantic studies in the literary academy and launched Frye as the pre-eminent English-speaking critic of his generation. Harold Bloom of Yale University, one of the most widely read critics of the generation after Frye's, told an interviewer several years ago that it had "ravished my heart away. I must have read it a hundred times between 1947 and 1950, probably intuitively memorized it, and will never escape the effect of it."[49]

One of the reasons *Fearful Symmetry* had to go through such a protracted labor was that its earlier drafts had contained not just a reading of Blake but also a good deal on the principles of literary symbolism by which Blake was to be understood. Only by pruning this theoretical luxuriance around Blake was Frye able to get his manuscript into a compact and coherent enough form to publish it. He intended to follow it with a book on Spenser, but the problem recurred. The theory by which he was explaining Spenser "obstinately adhered to a larger theoretical structure,"[50] until there was more and more about terms like *myth*, *symbol*, *ritual*, and *archetype* and less and less about Spenser himself. The result was *Anatomy of Criticism*, published in 1957 and still reverberating today.

The *Anatomy* laid out the ideas that would occupy Frye for the rest of his life. At the center of the work is what Frye called "the assumption of total coherence,"[51] the idea that literature can and should be considered as a whole and not just as an ever-expanding pile of individual works. Years before, while working on a graduate paper on Blake's poem *Milton*, he had suddenly seen how Blake and Milton both exist within the mythological framework of the Bible. The Bible, Frye saw, was a cosmos, a comprehensive body of stories and images within which a society lives. In the *Anatomy* he argued that the primitive stock of stories within any society will tend to clump together in a mythology and that this agglomerative tendency is inherent in the very existence of words. (On the question of the origin of myth he was equivocal: "If there is no sense that the mythological universe is a human creation, man can never get free of servile anxieties and superstitions . . . But, if there is no sense that it is also something uncreated, something coming from elsewhere, man remains a Narcissus staring at his own reflection.")[52] Literature in a sense is what happens to these stories, their further adventures as they evolve and are transformed. To account for these transformations, Frye borrowed the terms *condensation* and *displacement* from Freud's *Interpretation of Dreams*. For example, mythical structures appear in realistic fiction only in highly displaced forms.

Looking at literature this way yielded Frye a whole array of analytic and diagrammatic devices. There is a theory of modes that traces the descent of literature from myth, a theory of symbols that shows how works of art gather meaning for their readers, a theory of myths that describes the basic shapes of stories, and a theory of genres that distinguishes literary forms from each other. Hostile critics have seen in this schematic approach a stultifying system. Poet and playwrite James Reaney compares it to an amusement park — the circle of myths a ferris wheel, the theory of genres a roller coaster, and so on — and I find his whimsical comparison with its whiff of popcorn and whirling lights more apt to the exuberant generosity of Frye's intelligence than any suggestion of a closed system.[53]

Like Aristotle, whose durable categories of tragic flaw, recognition, catharsis, and so on still provide a common framework for comprehending tragedy,

Frye provides basic categories. Often the questions he invites are wonderfully simple: Are we looking up or down at the characters in a story? Is their power of action greater or less than our own? Does the action of the story rise or fall? As a young man, Frye comments in *The Educated Imagination*, "I thought little of fundamental questions because I assumed that anyone who asked them was naive. I think now that the simplest questions are not only the hardest to answer but the most important to ask."[54]

Frye began his *Anatomy* with what he aptly called a "Polemical Introduction." This was a witty and abrasive manifesto for a new criticism, written in a style so confident that it still gave me a sense of exhilaration verging on vertigo when I recently re-read it. Criticism, Frye says, is in a mess, plagued by amateurism and imported ideologies. Critics lack even elementary principles by which to distinguish verse from prose, literary from non-literary forms of writing, and various works of literature from each other. "The critical theory of genres," he says tartly, "is stuck precisely where Aristotle left it."[55] These principles, according to Frye, must be derived from literature itself and not imported from psychology, sociology, or theology.

Frye claims that criticism's lack of an independent discipline results from literature's lack of an independent social authority. Ever since Plato kicked the poets out of his ideal republic, he says, ideologues have tried to center literature outside itself, allowing it, as Horace says, "to delight and instruct" but keeping it subservient to religious, patriotic, or pedagogical goals. In his own time Frye sees the evidence of this in the influence of Thomist critics, Marxist critics, and psycholanalytic critics, all trying to explain and justify literature by an alien standard. Just as he himself had derived his knowledge of the principles of literary symbolism from his study of Blake, he says, so critical principles generally must come from an inductive survey of literature under the assumption of total coherence. Only then will criticism achieve "the sense of consolidating progress that belongs to a science."[56]

Frye challenges the image of the critic as a parasite who criticizes because he cannot create. "All the arts are dumb," he says, and involve "a disinterested use of words . . . The artist, as John Stuart Mill saw in a wonderful flash of critical insight, is not heard but overheard."[57] A poet cannot be explained by his background, his circumstances, or his intentions. He can be understood only as an aspect of poetry itself. It is the critic's job to display the total order within which the mute utterances of genius take their proper shape and place. To do this he must be guided by knowledge rather than taste. Taste is the province of the gentleman, "the public critic" or man of letters like Lamb or Arnold who shows "how literature is to be absorbed into society."[58] These critics show how literature is to be appreciated but not how it is to be understood. Taste is always limited by ideological preconceptions, according to Frye, and cannot provide criticism with a secure foundation. Whether a critic likes something should be of no more interest than whether a physicist prefers protons to neutrons.

A criticism that merely judges or merely classifies is still in the "state of naive induction which we find in primitive science":[59] it takes its structure from its own data, rather than providing an explanatory framework for those data. Like biology in the age of Linnaeus, it takes for granted precisely what it should explain. Frye did not explicitly identify himself as criticism's Darwin or the *Anatomy* as its *Origin of Species*, but it is clear that he thought he was doing something analogous. In seeing literature as "a complication of a relatively restricted and simple group of formulas,"[60] he intended a hypothesis comparable to the theory of evolution: a testable proposition that could begin to replace a criticism based on "ritual masonic gestures . . . too occult for syntax"[61] with verifiable knowledge.

Frye's desire to make criticism scientific rang alarm bells in the sacred precincts of humanism — and in a sense he did overlook his own myth of science in his rush to create a science of myth[62] — but it is clear, at least in retrospect, that he intended the idea analogically. He did not imagine that critical knowledge could ever have the same status as knowledge in the mathematical sciences, but he did think that if critics investigated literature as an "order of words" with an assumed coherence, they would be able, in effect, to crack its code. Indeed Frye had believed with Blake from the beginning that in Western civilization the Bible was this code.

Huston Smith once said of Darwin that his genius consisted in putting forward the only hypothesis that science, on its first principles, could make about the origin of species; and Thomas Henry Huxley, after the book's publication, is said to have re-marked, "Now why didn't we think of that?" Frye's ideas too had the quality of seeming obvious and astonishingly simple after they had first been ex-plained, but they arose as a response to a question about the nature of literature so simple and so seem-ingly naive that few others had bothered to ask it. Anyone who has negotiated the boundary between art and reality has shared the experience of the man in the Zen parable who dreamed he was a butterfly and then awoke and wondered if he might not be a butterfly dreaming he was a man. In the arts reality and illusion change places; the house lights go down and the stage lights come up. But often there comes a puzzling and melancholy moment at the end, when the reality of the illusion has not quite faded and the illusion of reality has not quite reasserted itself, and we have to ask ourselves what it means to have been so captivated by what is obviously no longer there. Frye does not idealize the experience of art — he knows, as he says, that we are always seeing *Hamlet* with a hangover or *King Lear* with an incompetent Cordelia — but he does explain why art matters. "A serious human life," he says, ". . . can hardly begin until we see an element of illusion in what is really there, and something real in fantasies about what might be there instead."[63]

Art is this play of possibilities, "a world of specu-lation," as Eliot says, in which "echoes inhabit the garden,"[64] and we experiment with what might be true. It draws the shapeless world of experience into the recurrent order of story and presents the unre-pressed form of what we love and what we hate, what we fear and what we desire. Literature, Frye says, is "a human apocalypse,"[65] which separates what we really care about from what social existence forces us to care about. According to Bert Hamilton, Frye frees his readers from the idea that aesthetic response is nothing more than "mindless consumption of pleasurable objects," a multiplication of "incommunicable appreciations."[66] Instead he shows works of art to be "ethical instruments, participating in the work of civilization."[67]

Literature for Frye is not an object to be appreciated but a power to be actively possessed by its readers. Blake says of the images of the Bible: "If the spectator could enter into these images in his imagination, approaching them on the fiery chariot of his contemplative thought, if he could enter into Noah's rainbow or into his bosom, or could make a friend and companion of one of these images of wonder which always entreats him to leave mortal things, then would he arise from his grave, then would he meet the Lord in the air, and then he would be happy."[68]

Frye believes that all literary images, however remotely, imitate this power. The archetypes of the literary imagination are vehicles. We must possess them as much as they possess us. The imagination by itself is "rigidly conventionalized"[69] — when are we less free than when we are in love or at war, transformed into mere automata of a story that seems to tell us? It is in the wrestle between the archetype and the individual life in which it is humanized and individuated that "the work of civilization" is done.

Northrop Frye never claimed originality for his ideas. He knew that while experience is always unique, knowledge is always recycled. Shelley had spoken in his *Defence of Poetry* of "that great poem, which all poets like the cooperating thoughts of one great Mind, have built up since the beginning of the world."[70] Frye said no more when he suggested that poetry is already latent in the very existence of words. Poetry is an intuition of what words can do, and the great poet is never entirely original but only more "profoundly imitative" than the mediocre poet.[71] What distinguished Frye was not that he said anything that poets hadn't always said but that he took what poets said seriously and claimed for it a social authority he felt it had always been denied.

After the publication of the *Anatomy* Frye developed an enormous following. At a special session of the English Institute devoted to Frye's work in 1965, American critic Murray Krieger said that Frye had had "an influence — indeed an absolute hold — on a generation of developing literary critics greater and more exclusive than that of any one theorist in recent cultural history."[72] But Frye also had his critics. Such poets as Irving Layton and Louis Dudek in Montreal found Frye's poetics stultifying. Layton, with his cult of the erotic and spontaneous, could not bear the suggestion that writers work largely with conventional materials, so he portrayed Frye as a desiccated academic: "Mr Butchevo Phrye/ Was born to pry,/ Among old bones/ And cemetery stones."[73] Dudek was more courteous than the sometimes vituperative Layton; but, with his own poetic roots in descriptive realism and Imagism's idealization of the unique and ineffable moment of perception, he still found Frye to be "the Great White Whale of Canadian criticism."[74]

Most criticisms of Frye revolved around the idea that he belonged to, or had invented, a mythopoetic school of criticism based on a claustral system that emphasized structure, pattern, and archetype to such an extent that it denied both the originality of artists and the social origins of their work. This view was aptly caught in a little piece of doggerel that circulated among the students at Victoria College in 1986. It was entitled "Reflections on Spending Three Straight Hours Reading *Anatomy of Criticism*." *Toronto* magazine later reprinted it under the headline "The Only Poem Northrop Frye Hasn't Read."

> Northrop Frye
> Whatta guy
> Read more books than you or I
> Treats them with an equal eye
> Archetypes are apple pie
> Will she cry? Will he die?
> Northrop never wonders why
> Shakespeare cannot make him shy
> Shylock's just like Captain Bligh
> Value judgments are a lie
> Find the patterns that apply
> Squeeze out *Hamlet*, let it dry
> Presto! *Catcher in the Rye*.[75]

Other criticisms of Frye were more elevated, but they usually sounded the same note. Psychoanalytic critics like Frederick Crews found that Frye obscured the origin of art "in discontent" by idealizing "the poet's wish for total imaginative control over the world" and perpetuating the "common fantasy among writers [that] art could be self-fathered, self-nurturing, self-referential [and] purified of its actual origins."[76] Neo-Marxist critics such as Frederic Jameson claimed that Frye had erased "the mark of ideology" from his system by projecting "the ideology of centralized and hieratic power societies back into myth."[77] The disciples of Jacques Derrida called him logocentric if not, in the master's later formulation, phallogocentric.

Frye remained largely impervious to these criticisms. He never entered into argument with his critics, believing their assumptions to be too remote from his own to allow for dialogue, and generally restricted himself to the occasional weary or withering aside. In the 1970s he found criticism "still mired in ideology," and in the 80s he alluded to "the wasteland of critical theory" and prayed for an end to the current "plague of darkness."[78] Certainly the great expectations he expressed in his "Polemical Introduction" went unfulfilled. Fad succeeded fad, and criticism continued to be "swept with confused alarms of struggle and flight," never developing that equable sense of "consolidating progress" for which he had hoped.

Frye toward the end of his life must have had the curious experience of feeling both lionized and ignored, his celebrity serving almost as an inoculation against his teaching. But he had always stood in an ambiguous relation to his times. In one sense he

virtually wrote criticism's declaration of independence and so prepared the way for contemporary
Critical Theory, which sometimes seems to have
swallowed both literature and philosophy whole.
Frye not only shared but contributed to the emphasis on language in twentieth-century thought.
Whether in suggesting that poems are latent in the
order of words, or in saying that words turn their
backs on the world to compose their own self-contained grammatical fictions, or in suggesting that
words use us as much as we use them, Frye shares
in the contemporary consensus that language, as
Heidegger says, is the House of Being. But Frye also
stood aside from his time, distinguished by his evan-
gelical attitude and by what Donald Riccomini calls
"the playful, open unrepressed presence in his work
of the transcendental."[79] Because he believed that
the world originates in the utterance of a divine
Word, he escaped the nihilistic conclusion that the
systemic, self-enclosed, and self-referential character of language points to its being, if not arbitrary
and ultimately meaningless, at least without origin
or end.

In 1964, a year before Frye was honored by the
English Institute, French philosopher Jacques
Derrida gave a paper at Johns Hopkins University
in Baltimore called "Structure, Sign and Play in the
Discourse of the Human Sciences."[80] It announced
the arrival in literary studies of deconstruction, although Derrida did not use that word, and the beginning of a movement that would eventually usurp
Frye's pre-eminence in the world of literary criticism. In his paper Derrida took on structuralism and

argued that it necessarily exempted the idea of structure itself — "the structure of structure" — from scrutiny. He suggested that in any system of thought there is always an explicit or implied center. "The center," he said, "is at the center of the totality and yet, since the center does not belong to the totality . . . the totality has its center elsewhere." The moment that Nietzsche announced as the death of God was the recognition that there is no center. From that moment, Derrida said,

> the center could not be thought in the form of a being present [and so became] a sort of non-locus in which an infinite number of sign-substitutions came into play. This moment was that in which language invaded the universal problematic; that in which, in the absence of a center or origin, everything became discourse . . . that is to say, when everything became a system where the central signified, the original or transcendental signified, is never absolutely present outside a system of differences. The absence of the transcendental signified extends the domain and the interplay of signification *ad infinitum.*

The center that disappears as a presence but persists as a function in Derrida's thought is whatever gives meaning and so escapes analysis as meaning. It is Eliot's "still point of the turning world."[81] The recognition of "broken immediateness" can take the melancholy form of what George Steiner calls "nostalgia for the absolute"[82] or the affirmative form of Nietzsche's embrace of humanity's freedom to make meaning in the absence of truth. The center persists only as function and as "trace." Tracing this trace involves an infinite series of deconstructions, in which meaning ceaselessly chases its own tail. Because thought is impossible without the functional concept of a center, the idea of a center can never be overcome but only endlessly deconstructed. (This is the characteristic postmodern posture, which Derrida calls "rupture and redoubling.")

Derrida and Frye have an interesting relationship as much because of the similarity as because of the differences in their thought; and, in Frye's occasional writings of the 1980s, collected in the volume *Myth and Metaphor*, Derrida is a significant "trace," often alluded to but never struck more than a glancing blow. Frye too acknowledges that there is nothing outside the text, and that the Bible, for example, points at no "transcendental signified" existing outside its pages. But he also believes that within the text we encounter "the power of the genuine Word and Spirit, the power that has created all our works of culture and imagination, and is still ready to recreate both our society and ourselves."[83]

For Frye the text of the Bible is not, as with Derrida, "an absence invoking a presence" but the place where that presence is continually recreated. Frye acknowledges a process of decreation analogous to Derrida's deconstruction, in which the free play of the imagination subverts the hypnotic power of "objective" reality, but he also acknowledges the process of recreation in which a voice speaks once again from the burning bush in the desert. The Logos, for Frye, is always imaginatively recreated, never an objective truth, and at the same time always more than we can imagine. Nevertheless the Incarnational Word exists, and this gives Frye's thought a serene and lucent confidence that is in very marked contrast to Derrida's edgy verbal pyrotechnics and Sisyphean heroics. Derrida and Frye in a sense represent the poles of possible response to the modern crisis: the abandonment of Christianity or its imaginative reconstruction.

Derrida was the door through which the heirs of Nietzsche infiltrated contemporary North American literary criticism and dashed Frye's hopes that criticism could become "the pioneer of education and the shaper of cultural tradition."[84] Frye says in one of his late essays that through the lens of current critical theory culture today seems to be "a vast chaos of *écriture* where there are no boundary lines between literature and anything else in words."[85] By failing to distinguish literature from "the vast chaos of *écriture*" that appears when "everything becomes discourse," deconstruction denied literature the social authority with which Frye had hoped to imbue it. And by writing in an opaque and technical style, deconstructive critics also undermined Frye's hope that criticism could address a broad literate public. Frye valued plain expression — a colleague once said that the questions Frye was asked after a lecture amounted to saying, "I think you've explained that a little too clearly; would you mind clouding it up a bit."[86] The writing style of the new critics, Frye said, reminded him "of a horse slurping water."

Derrida's influence also tended to take criticism out of literature, where Frye had hoped to establish it, and into philosophy. Frye was a critic who thought "as poets think, in terms of metaphor," and who once said that the creation of a poem is ideally the same thing as the theory by which it is created. ("Creative effort is inseparable from the awareness of what it is doing.")[87] By establishing criticism within literature he hoped to enhance the value of specifically literary forms of expression. Deconstruction once again preferred to associate criticism with "some Herculean force" outside literature rather than patiently explicating literature from within its boundaries.[88] Frye never explicitly fought back but was not above the occasional tart remark: "I now frequently encounter objections to my alleged passion for ticketing and labelling things where reference to an excessive toilet training in my infancy is clearly being suppressed with some reluctance. But when I turn to other areas of critical theory and am informed, for example, that the privileging of interdiscursivity problematizes the differentializing of contextuality, I do not feel I am being released from an obsession. I only feel that I am facing different conventions about what it is important to find names for."[89]

In the last ten years of his life Frye published three books about the Bible: *The Great Code*, *Words with Power*, and the posthumous *The Double Vision*, which he said he intended as "a shorter and more accessible version" of the first two. These books fleshed out ideas that had been embryonically present in his writing since *Fearful Symmetry*. Frye had been teaching a course on the Bible since the early 1940s, and the *Anatomy* acknowledged Blake's idea that "The

Old and New Testaments are the Great Code of Art."[90] In these final works he developed his reading of the Bible and his philosophy of language at length and left a legacy that will eventually be of as much interest to theologians as to students of literature.

Frye did not write as a theologian; and, by giving *The Great Code* the subtitle *The Bible and Literature*, he made it plain that he was not appropriating the Bible *as* literature. Instead, he borrowed from Rudolf Bultmann the Greek word *kerygma*, or proclamation, to describe the Bible's unique status as a written text. But he did argue that the Bible is written in literary figures and addressed to the imagination. And, although Frye claimed competence only in literary criticism, not in philosophy or theology, he found both fields to be fair game once they were imported into criticism. (The point of scholarship, Frye said, is not to make a fruitless effort to know everything but to treat your specialty as the center of all knowledge. "For a contemporary critic interested in Freud or Wittgenstein or Lévi-Strauss, such writers, like medieval angels, do not travel through space from another subject: they manifest themselves from within his subject.")[91]

Frye begins *The Great Code* by dividing language into three phases: the metaphoric, the metonymic, and the descriptive, each requiring to be understood in its own way. When Jesus, for example, says, "I am the vine, ye are the branches," as he does in the Gospel of John, his meaning can be discerned only metaphorically or, in St. Paul's word, spiritually. He is neither saying that he is like a vine, or that a vine is an emblem that can represent him, but that he and the vine are exchangeably identified, and their meanings inherent in each other. (It is this metaphorical interpenetration that culminates in giant forms like Milton's Christian Commonwealth, Rilke's angel, or Frye's own image of literature as "a mythical and metaphorical organism.")[92] Distinguishing three phases of language allows Frye to make distinctions that are usually missed about the word *God*. When we ask whether God exists, for example, are we asking about the God who *is* a vine, or about the God of the theologians whose nature can be reasoned about (as when St. Thomas says in the *Summa Contra Gentiles* that God hates nothing even though he knows that in the Old Testament God hates plenty of things)? Or are we asking about a God whose existence any conceivable form of science could prove or disprove? Metaphoric and metonymic language both carry their proper conception of God — descriptive language cannot form one because God is not an object that can be represented. So when Nietzsche says that God is dead, or the French astronomer Laplace that God is a hypothesis of which he no longer has any need, neither is making statements about God as such but only about how God is perceived within a certain linguistic framework. The God who is dead because he cannot be discerned within a disenchanted and descriptively rendered nature is for Frye not dead at all but only "entombed in a dead language."[93]

At no point in *The Great Code* does Frye directly challenge dogmatic theology, but it is clear enough that there is no room for orthodoxy or reasoned arguments about what "must be true" in his approach to religion. Frye approaches the Bible as myth, and myth as what is both more and less true than ordinary experience. Myth is what might be true or could be made true. Faith involves first of all accepting the reality of the imagination — a reality that is "proved" by the organic unity of literature — and then putting this reality to the test to find out how real it is. "In proportion as subject and object become illusory," says Frye, "the world of intelligibility connecting them becomes reality."[94] ("None by travelling over known lands can find out the unknown," is Blake's axiom.[95] "The assertion 'I believe that' is not simply meaningless but actively dangerous when we still don't know who 'I' is or what 'that' is," adds Frye.)[96] The test of the imagination's truth is in experience. We meet God as a person because that is all we are capable of knowing. If we claim to believe what we have not tested, or erect a God who is more than a person, we are ensnared in what Blake calls "the net of religion" and liable to be ground in the gears of our own inhuman idols.

Frye's way of reading the Bible points to what he calls an "open community" of vision.[97] This contrasts with the closed community that forms when "professed belief" hardens into enforced ideology. It also points a way beyond religious and ideological rivalries, and a way of disengaging the question of what we know from the question of what we belong to. When faith is defined as "whatever consistency one's behaviour exhibits throughout one's life,"[98] or as "a continuous sequence of committed acts guided by a vision,"[99] a criterion of truth exists which is beyond belief. "Reason, or the ratio of all that we have already known," says Blake, "is not the same that it shall be when we know more."[100] Placing the center of religion in imaginative response creates a community with an open horizon and allows particular faiths to interpenetrate without contradiction.

Following its publication in 1982, *The Great Code* received a number of interesting reviews. *The Globe and Mail* had the perversely inspired idea of giving it to George Grant. Grant sputtered inconclusively about Frye as a modern, secularized, and scientized Protestant and seemed by the end to have virtually accused him of atheism.[101] It was also twice discussed in the pages of the *Toronto Journal of Theology*, where the two views advanced seemed the poles of possible theological response to Frye's ideas. William Fennell was uneasy with what he felt was Frye's denial of "the objective reality of God" and his "idealization of reality."[102] Against Frye's assertion that "the Bible is explicitly anti-referential in structure and deliberately blocks off a world of presence behind itself,"[103] Fennell argued that "the Bible points to a reality other than itself." Donald Wiebe, on the other hand, suggested that, if theology wants to escape a situation in which a "neatly packaged . . . system of doctrines . . . inevitably fall[s] prey to the superior cognitive power of the sciences," it should accept that refusing "to seek a meaning for God outside the language context . . . in which [the word] is found may be the only adequate theology to be had."[104] What is interesting is not just the apparent difference of opinion here but also the fact that

Frye's work has begun to inspire interesting questions within theology about how Christianity is to be taught and celebrated when it is understood as a myth addressed to the imagination and not as "an objective reality."

It is my view that Frye's work is likely to be seen in future as having implications in many fields. To choose only one example, I think Frye has something to say to an environmental movement now split between "deep ecologists" who want to reenchant nature, and reform ecologists who adjust themselves to utilitarian rationales in order to bring about practical changes. Frye distinguishes between an objective nature, which is a mechanism indifferent to our purposes, and an imagined nature in which "the morning stars sing together" and "the mountains clap hands for joy." And he insists that the difference between the two is in us and not in nature. The fall in Genesis is a fall into an objective nature, a creation in which we have not participated. The awakened imagination must "decreate" this fallen world in order to become itself a participant in creation. The neolithic goddesses and revived nature gods that populate the farther reaches of "environmental consciousness" symbolize a state in which we remain unborn within nature and the passive object of our own projected emotions. Frye points out an alternative to this reactionary stance. He recognizes that it is just as evil to exploit nature as to exploit another human being but only because nature is our fellow creature, not because either is divine. In *Myth and Metaphor* he cites the Zen Buddhist saying "First there is a tree and a mountain;

then there is no tree and no mountain; then there is a tree and a mountain."[105] This corresponds to Frye's three stages of creation-decreation-recreation. The final mountain is "a creation in which we have participated." Instead of succumbing to an idolatry of nature, "imagination passes beyond the empty heavens into its original earth."[106]

Running through the works of the second half of Frye's life is a vision of what he came to call primary concern. The primary concerns of human beings are things like food, sex, property, and freedom, the things we want most and yet most often sacrifice at the thrones and altars of what Frye called secondary concern. Ideological concerns are secondary, but they frequently dominate social life. Literature, according to Frye, is always an expression of primary concern. It may contain ideas, but these will always subserve a more rudimentary structure of hope and desire. Henry James created extraordinarily complex and ethereal fictions but was said to have "a mind so fine that no idea could violate it" because the warp on which these fictions were woven was still the subtle structure of his characters' desires.[107] Art and religion, for Frye, are both visions of gratified desire and a world in human form.

Vaclav Havel, in his essay "Stories and Totalitarianism," contrasts the liberating power of stories with the repressive power of totalitarian ideologies.[108] He defines stories as conflicts between separate or previously unrelated realities — "the incursion of one logic into the world of another logic." Stories imply plurality and, like games, uncertainty as to how they will turn out. None of the competing actors have truth; truth exists only in the story as a whole and is therefore a vision possessed only by the listener or reader. Totalitarianism he defines by contrast as a state in which everything is already known, one agent monopolizes truth, and stories are by definition impossible. Frye draws a similar distinction between ideology and myth. Myth, he says, sets up a counter-environment through which the hopes and fears we have screened out of our lives can re-enter social existence. In social intercourse, says Frye, we prefer to say the right thing rather than tell the truth. Imagination is the leaven that prevents the collapse of convention into cliché and reminds us of "the society we want to live in."[109] Like Havel's stories, which subvert totalitarian designs because we don't know how they will turn out, literature keeps a vision of what we want alive in the midst of what we have had to settle for. "I see it as the essential task of the literary critic," he says, "to distinguish ideology from myth, to help reconstitute myth as a language, and to put literature in its proper place as the central link of communication between society and the vision of its primary concerns."[110]

Northrop Frye was a tremendously hopeful thinker. He harbored few illusions about human nature — he called the century through which he had lived a "phantasmagoria"[111] and man without God "a psychotic ape"[112] — and yet he never forgot that in an instant everything could be different.

I think immense changes could be brought about by a Christianity that was no longer a ghost with

the chains of a foul historical record of cruelty
clanking behind it . . . Such a Christianity might
represent the age of the Spirit that the thirteenth-
century Franciscan Joachim of Floris saw as su-
perceding the Old Testament age of the Father
and the New Testament age of the Logos. It would
be a Christianity of a Father who is not a metaphor
of male supremacy but the intelligible source of
our being; of a Son who is not a teacher of plati-
tudes but a Word who has overcome the world;
and of a Spirit who speaks with all the tongues of
men and angels and still speaks with charity. The
Spirit of creation who brought life out of chaos
brought death out of it too, for death is all that
makes sense of life in time. The Spirit that broods
on the chaos of our psyches brings to birth a body
that is in time and history but not enclosed by
them, and is in death only because it is in the midst
of life as well.[113]

I
MONCTON AND
METHODISM

DAVID CAYLEY: I would like to begin by asking how your religious and cultural background shaped your vocation.

NORTHROP FRYE: I think my religious background really did shape almost everything. It gave me the mythological framework I was brought up inside of, and I know from experience that once you're inside a mythological framework you can't break outside of it. You can alter or adapt it to yourself, but it's always there.

CAYLEY: Can you say what it was? What was, or is, Methodism?

FRYE: I think Methodism is an approach to Christianity that puts a very heavy emphasis on the quality of experience. That is one reason why I've always tended to think in terms of, first, a myth that repeats itself over and over again through time, and, second, the experience which is the response to it. Nothing that happens in history is unique. Everything is part of turning cycles or mythical repetition. Everything in experience is unique. I think it was because of the emphasis on the uniqueness of experience I acquired so early that I realized the other half of this was the mythological pattern.

CAYLEY: The emphasis on experience in Methodism — can you contrast that with other approaches to Christianity?

FRYE: The Catholic approach, for example, is very much more doctrinal. You learn a structure of doctrine, you step inside it, and the doctrine performs instead of the myth. In Methodism you listen to the stories of the Bible. As Presbyterians used to say, the reason why Methodist ministers moved every two years was that the structure of doctrine in Methodism was totally exhausted long before then.

CAYLEY: What were the historical conditions under which Methodism arose?

FRYE: It arose as a Canadian resistance to British and French establishments. There was a Roman Catholic establishment in Quebec, and a Church of England and a Presbyterian one in Ontario. Methodism moved in as part of a native protest. And of course the only place from which the influence could come was the United States.

CAYLEY: How was this manifest in your particular background?

FRYE: My mother's father was a Methodist circuit-rider. He always stayed in country areas because he was so innocent. He always thought that the place he was assigned was the place that God had called him to, and he didn't realize that he was in with a bunch of pushing entrepreneurs who were grabbing all the soft spots in the bigger cities.

CAYLEY: Did you know him well?

FRYE: No. He died when I was about nine years old, and I wasn't connected with him after about four or five. What I know of him is what I picked up from the family.

CAYLEY: There's an image in John Ayre's biography of you clutching your copy of *Pilgrim's Progress* like a teddy bear.[114] Is this fanciful or not?

FRYE: It was partly the Methodist blue Sunday, where you couldn't do anything on Sunday except read. I had a whole shelf full of children's adaptations of the classics, and the *Pilgrim's Progress* was one thing that most homes, like the one I was brought up in, encouraged the reading of.

CAYLEY: But would you have been steeped in that book?

FRYE: Well, it was there.

CAYLEY: You grew up in Moncton?

FRYE: I was born in Sherbrooke, and when my father's business failed, we moved to Lennoxville, about three miles away. I stayed there until I was about seven or eight. Then my father became a hardware salesman for the Maritimes and settled in Moncton because it was central for his travelling. So I moved to Moncton when I was about eight.

CAYLEY: And did you feel like an exile when you went to Moncton?

FRYE: My parents did, and I suppose I caught it from them. I was too young to feel that I was an exile, but they lost all their friends and never felt accepted in the Maritimes.

CAYLEY: To the very end?

FRYE: Of course, other things happened. My father was always of a rather retiring disposition socially. He was affable enough with people, but he wasn't a socializer. And my mother got extremely deaf and withdrawn and introverted. I was really brought up by grandparents, in effect. That is, I was born when my mother was over forty. My father's business had failed, my older brother had been killed in the First World War, and we were in a new community where they were too old to adapt — my mother was deaf. I always felt there was a kind of generation gap there.

CAYLEY: And a remoteness from the society you were living in?

FRYE: Yes, both from that and even from my parents themselves, because they belonged to a previous generation more dramatically than most parents do with their children.

CAYLEY: How did this affect you?

FRYE: It made me extremely introverted and drawn in on myself. You see, I was brought up not only psychologically as a grandchild but also as an "only" child. I did have one sister, but she was twelve years older and so of another generation. I was very much thrown in on myself. And being temperamentally extremely bookish and rather awkward physically made me even more so.

CAYLEY: What part did imagination play in your life?

FRYE: I suppose it was always there. It was a matter of becoming more and more aware of it. I should have added that along with the introverted temperament, there was also the fact that our family was in a state of shabby genteel poverty the whole time. I simply could not afford the freedom of social movement that other boys had. So, to some extent, I lived in an imaginary dream world. I suppose most children do. I was very much lacking in practical skills and social savoir faire. Because of that I suppose I spent the first seventeen years of my life mooning. When there is no world to live in except the world of the imagination, naturally that's going to take shape.

CAYLEY: How did it take shape for you as a child? Do you remember?

FRYE: I suppose it took shape as a world to become a writer in. My first impulses were the writing of fiction, and I kept writing fiction. For some reason or other I was born without the poetic faculty, or at least I never seemed to have much affinity for that. But for prose fiction I did, because that was what I was reading. It didn't take me long to discover that that wasn't my field either.

CAYLEY: How did you first get to Toronto?

FRYE: The typing contest. That's part of the Frye saga. I went to business college after high school. The Underwood Typewriter Company was running a typing contest in Toronto, and I got my fare paid, which was quite a consideration.

CAYLEY: I can't pretend not to know this story. You placed second, I think.

FRYE: In the Canadian one, yes. I didn't do so well in the North American one.

CAYLEY: How old would you have been then?

FRYE: I was sixteen for the Canadian contest in the spring and seventeen in the fall, when I went to college.

CAYLEY: And you travelled alone to Toronto?

FRYE: Yes.

CAYLEY: Do you remember that journey?

FRYE: Oh, yes. I remember several journeys. I took one to Chicago to see my sister when I was fourteen. They made a very considerable impression on me.

CAYLEY: How?

FRYE: I don't know. It's hard to pin it down. It was the feeling of drifting through the landscape in this immense space and the darkness gradually closing in and gradually lightening up again. I think I've recorded, too, the view of Quebec in the early dawn from the Lévis side of the St. Lawrence. But it was not as overwhelming as the ship voyage coming in through the Gulf of St. Lawrence and then down the river. That was something utterly unforgettable.

CAYLEY: You were seventeen when you went to Victoria College?

FRYE: Yes.

CAYLEY: I have the impression you found it quite liberating.

FRYE: It was tremendous, because I was in a society where I felt I had a function. But there were many awkwardnesses at first, because I was from the Maritimes and I was quite different from the Ontario boys. I had to become like them as fast as possible.

CAYLEY: How different?

FRYE: Oh, they wore hats and I wore a cap. These were trifles, but my general attitude was different partly because the high school in Moncton was so primitive in the twenties, and they had all had a very much better education. They were grade thirteen and I was grade eleven, plus business college.

II
CRITICAL BEGINNINGS

CAYLEY: When did you begin reading Blake?

FRYE: I think I began reading Blake in Pelham Edgar's Shakespeare class, which he taught very badly because he didn't like Shakespeare. He's the only professor of English I ever knew who didn't like Shakespeare. Victoria College being what it was, he got the Shakespeare course to teach, but he was always talking about other things, usually about contemporary Canadian poets. He did mention Blake in a way that aroused my curiosity, so I looked into him. This was in my second year as an undergraduate. In my third year I took the eighteenth-century course with him, and he assigned me a paper on Blake. From then on I was hooked.

CAYLEY: Did you see right away that you had found your teacher in Blake?

FRYE: Not right away. But here was a fascinating character that very little had been said about. Two years later, after my graduation, I was at Emmanuel, where Herbert Davis, who was a Swift scholar in the graduate school, gave a course on Blake, and I signed up for it. I was assigned a paper on Blake's *Milton*, one of his most difficult and complex poems, and started working on it the night before I was to read it. It was around three in the morning when suddenly the universe just broke open, and I've never been, as they say, the same since.

CAYLEY: What was it? I know you can't describe the experience, but what was it in Blake that provoked this experience?

FRYE: Just the feeling of an enormous number of things making sense that had been scattered and unrelated before. In other words, it was a mythological frame taking hold.

CAYLEY: A conversion?

FRYE: Conversions usually relate to the other side, the experience. As a Methodist I was brought up converted. I never went through a conversion process.

CAYLEY: A reconversion?

FRYE: Well, it was really getting the other half of what conversion is about.

CAYLEY: What provoked it?

FRYE: The feeling that here I was dealing with an extremely complex poem of Blake's about Milton, with whom he obviously had a very close, intricate love-hate relationship. Toward the end, I had the feeling that what united Blake and Milton, for all their differences — one was a Puritan and the other was very much an eighteenth-century nonconformist — was their common dependence on the Bible and the fact that the Bible had a framework of mythology that both Milton and Blake had entered into. Of course, by that time I'd shucked all the anxiety side of the religion I was brought up in.

CAYLEY: What actually happened that night?

FRYE: I don't know that I can say what it was. But it was an experience of things fitting together. I've had two or three nights where I've had sudden visions of that kind, visions ultimately of what I myself might be able to do. *Fearful Symmetry*, for example, was started innumerable times, but the shape of the whole book dawned on me quite suddenly one night. And the same thing happened once when I was staying in the YMCA in Edmonton, where I was for very dubious reasons reading Spengler's *Decline of the West*, and I suddenly got a vision of coherence. That's the only way I can describe it. Things began to form patterns and make sense.

CAYLEY: You say that by then you had already shucked the anxiety side of the religion you were brought up in. There's a remarkable letter in John Ayre's biography in which you say that you remember "walking along St. George Street . . . and just suddenly that whole shitty and smelly garment [of fundamentalist teaching I had all of my life] just dropped off into the sewers and stayed there."[115] Was this earlier?

FRYE: Yes, this was earlier, when I was still in high

school. As I realize now, I wasn't really brought up with that garment on me at all. Mother told me a lot of nonsense because her father had told it to her, and she thought it must be true and that it was her duty to pass it on. But something else came through, and you know how quick children are at picking up the overtones in what's said to them rather than what is actually said. I realize that Mother didn't really believe any of this stuff herself.

CAYLEY: But was unable to say so?

FRYE: She thought she did believe it. She thought she ought to believe it. But I can see now that as a child I picked up the tone of common sense behind it. Mother had a lot of common sense in spite of all that stuff.

CAYLEY: What was the garment that fell away?

FRYE: Oh, the anxieties about the old stinker in the sky and the postmortem hell and all the other anxieties that I was brought up with. I felt like the man in *1984* when he walked into the room of the man who had the privilege of turning off the telescreen. The old stinker up in the sky was not only dead, he was never there. My attitude, I'm afraid, was always the opposite of Newman's "Lead, Kindly Light," where he says "I loved to choose and see my path" and calls that pride.[116] Well, I always wanted to choose and see my path and was convinced that that was what God wanted too, and that if I went on with this "Lead Thou me on" routine I would run into spiritual gravitation and fall over a cliff.

CAYLEY: There's another letter to a friend in which you say from that day forth you resolved to take only what you could use from religion. I find it remarkable that at that age you could see it so clearly.

FRYE: Yes, I had no use for compulsory doctrines after that.

CAYLEY: And you really were from that time forward free from anxiety in relation to God?

FRYE: I think so, pretty free, and I was also relieved from the anxiety of having to rebel against what I'd been taught.

CAYLEY: The remarkable part of this for me is that you stopped arguing so young. It must have given you a remarkable freedom to get on with your work.

FRYE: Yes, it did.

CAYLEY: Your experience with Blake's *Milton* was many years before *Fearful Symmetry* actually came out. When did you begin writing the book? When did you know you were going to go as deeply into Blake as you did?

FRYE: About the time that I was writing that graduate paper, I started to make some tentative scribbles. I knew that I was going to write a book on Blake sooner or later, but I had both graduate courses and the Emmanuel theological course to get rid of first. Then I had to go to Oxford for two years, where I reread the English school, because I knew I wanted to teach English then. With three years of theology, I was getting rusty on English, so that hard program of reading rather kept the Blake on the back burner, although I did have a large pile of manuscript when I was an undergraduate at Oxford. When I came back, I had to get all those courses in a condition so that I could teach. I came back in the fall of 1939. The train got into Toronto the day the Soviet-Nazi pact was signed, and the next day one of my colleagues who taught the eighteenth century signed up, so I had that course to do as well as the three that I'd been assigned. Preparing for lectures really took all of the energy I had until about 1941, I think it was, when I began to write the book seriously. Then I struggled through the whole process. The book had five complete rewritings of which the third and fourth were half again as long as the published book.

CAYLEY: This is a ridiculous question to ask about a book of four hundred closely argued pages, but what was it you wanted to say about Blake that hadn't been said?

FRYE: I wanted to show that Blake was inside this mythological framework that I have been trying to outline ever since. I was trying to explain that framework along with Blake, and of course that made an absolutely impossible book.

CAYLEY: Why was it impossible?

FRYE: It was just too long and complex for any reader to dig his way through. I owe the reader at Princeton University Press, Carlos Baker, a great deal, in that he actually went through that chaos of manuscript and saw that it was totally unpublishable in that form, but that there was something there to retrieve. So I retrieved the Blake and left the rest until I wrote the *Anatomy of Criticism*.

CAYLEY: What was the rest?

FRYE: Some of it comes out in the *Anatomy of Criticism*, such as the historical modes and the circle of myths. The connection with the Bible, while it was very obvious in my mind, didn't come very explicitly into the *Anatomy*. It comes out in *The Great Code* and in the book I've just got through with now, *Words with Power*.

CAYLEY: What were the critical principles you got from Blake?

FRYE: The general assumption when I began as a critic was that you started with literal meaning, which is what Jacques Derrida calls the transcendental signified.[117] That is, there's something standing outside the Bible or whatever it is, and the words point to it and, when Christianity began saying "In the beginning was the Word," it was really warning against that kind of procedure, which of course Christianity promptly ignored and ignored totally for eighteen centuries. Blake was, it seems to me, again the first person to bring religion back to this "In the beginning was the Word." There's nothing outside the text.

CAYLEY: What did the Bible mean to Blake?

FRYE: The Bible to Blake was really the Magna Carta of the human imagination. It was the book that told man that he was free to create and imagine and that the power to create and imagine was ultimately the divine in man, that Christianity (and of course it's the Christian Bible Blake is talking about) was pre-eminently the religion which united the divine and the human and consequently opened a path of freedom to man which is infinite.

CAYLEY: In "The Everlasting Gospel" Blake says, "Thou art a man, God is no more, thine own humanity learn to adore."

FRYE: The Gospels represent Jesus as saying that nobody can understand God except through him, that is, except through the God-man. So you have

God and you have God-man and you have man and, if you try to approach God without the idea of the humanity of God, then you get what he calls old Nobodaddy, the ferocious old bugger up in the sky with the whiskers and the reactionary political views, who enjoys sending people to hell. And if you turn to man simply as man, then of course you're involved in all the evil that makes man a psychotic ape, and that's the tendency that he calls deism — that is, the tendency to substitute the totalitarian for the social. If you have the God-man, then you have both the divine and the human united in a single place. If you insist on separating God from man, you have merely God who is a scarecrow in the sky and merely man who is a psychotic ape.

CAYLEY: So when he says God is no more, he's not saying what it might at first seem.

FRYE: He is really saying that this *more* cannot be approached directly. You have to approach it through your own humanity. The human cannot really comprehend the non-human, or what transcends the human.

CAYLEY: Some have thought to find an atheist in Blake. Altizer, for example, wrote of this in the sixties.[118]

FRYE: There is no atheism in Blake, because that means that God is not personal. For Blake a God that is not personal is nothing at all.

CAYLEY: So it's the objectivity of God that he denies?

FRYE: It's the impersonality of God that he denies. He says that man can worship only two persons. If he doesn't worship God, he will worship, well, somebody like Hitler or Stalin — in other words, Antichrist.

CAYLEY: He also says that man in his creative acts and perceptions is God, or so you paraphrase him.

FRYE: Yes. For him everything that God does comes through man — the consciousness and the imagination of man. But you can't say that man is God. What you say is that God becomes man in order that we may be as he is. When Blake said that, he was, whether he knew it or not, quoting verbatim from St. Athanasius.

CAYLEY: Do you think he did know it?

FRYE: It's possible that he knew it. It's always a very dicey thing to say that Blake didn't know about something.

CAYLEY: I can remember Kathleen Raine saying that she set out as a young woman to read the books that Blake had read and found herself as an old woman still reading.[119]

FRYE: In my opinion Blake read the first twenty pages of a lot of books, but he had one hell of a struggle to get to page twenty-one. By that time his own desire to say what he had to say took over. The only books that he seems to have read with some thoroughness were books he hated and disliked, so that he could write curses in the margins.

CAYLEY: What did Blake mean by vision?

FRYE: He meant the capacity to live with one's eyes and ears in what he calls a spiritual world. It was not a world of ideas, it was not a Platonic world, it was a physical world in its organized form. He says, "Spirits are organized men." He also says, "A Spirit and a Vision are not . . . a cloudy vapour," or anything fuzzy.[120] They are organized and minutely articulated beyond anything the physical world can produce. In other words, it was his world of poetry and painting. Vision was for him, as I say, the ability to see and hear in that world.

CAYLEY: This was not a world that had an independent existence?

FRYE: Oh, no. This is the world as it really is, not the world as our lazy minds and senses perceive it.

CAYLEY: But in the act of vision one creates or organizes this world?

FRYE: One creates in order to have evidence that one does see and hear that way. The kinds of things that people used to get out of LSD visions are a kind of parody of what Blake was talking about. You see the world that's there, but you see it with an intensity and a clarity that, as I say, most people are too indolent to bother with.

CAYLEY: Where were his feet while he was hearing and seeing these things?

FRYE: They were on the ground mostly, because you have to sit down to paint and write poetry. But in a spiritual sense, they were dancing.

CAYLEY: George Goyder said to me that only Blake could paint people in midair and have them be plausible, and that when Fuseli or other contemporaries did it, they looked ridiculous.[121]

FRYE: There are quite a lot of Blake things at the Fogg Museum at Harvard, and the woman who ran it when I first went there said that of the people who came in to look at the Blake drawings perhaps the largest single group were students of ballet.

CAYLEY: You begin *Fearful Symmetry* with Blake's

theory of knowledge and his attack on the unholy trinity of Bacon, Newton and Locke, who often appear together in his writings as a sort of three-headed monster. What did he have against them?

FRYE: They all represent what most people now attach to Descartes. That is, a theory of a conscious ego which is an observer of the world but not a participant in it and that consequently regards the world as something to be dominated and mastered. That is, his real hatred of what he calls Bacon, Newton and Locke is based on what is ultimately a political feeling, that this kind of thing leads to the exploitation of nature and, as an inevitable by-product, the exploitation of other people.

CAYLEY: This is what he calls the cloven fiction, two-horned reasoning.

FRYE: By cloven fiction he means the Cartesian tendency to preserve the subject as something absolutely separate from the object. Man is not a subject separate from a natural object, he *is* a natural object, and things only get serious when the subject and the object get together and become unified. The notion of the subject as passive, collecting impressions from the outside world, struck him as abhorrent. It isn't that the creative person sees what isn't there; it's just that he sees what is there with his own distinctive power. He says that you are mutilating your own life if you are isolating the pure sense experience and classifying it rationally, that is that the emotional elements in sense experience are just as real, that you can't think of reality in a sterilized or antiseptic context as something that has escaped from the emotional. The real conventionally means what is out there and therefore can't be changed, but ninety per cent of our encounter with reality is an encounter with human rubbish, with what man has already made and has no longer much use for, and Blake, like Vico in Italy before him, is saying that in fact reality is what you make and you can't understand what you haven't made. But it's not a subjective making.

CAYLEY: Blake speaks in his poem *Milton* of "casting off the rotten rags of memory by inspiration." What is his distinction between memory and imagination?

FRYE: He's really the first person to use *imagination* in its positive, creative sense, as the later romantics, Coleridge and those people, did. Previously, imagination had meant what it meant to Shakespeare's Theseus in *Midsummer Night's Dream*, as seeing something that isn't there, what we would call the imaginary rather than the imaginative. The memory for him is again the tendency in the mind that we would call superstition. That is, a superstitious person is a person who does things because they have been done without having any knowledge of why they should be done, or why he's doing them. In a way, it's a rather misleading use of the term *memory*. There are two forms of memory: There is one where you're just brooding on the specters of the past, which is what he condemns, and there is another memory, which is the practice memory, and he's all for that. He says you can't learn to paint unless you do a lot of slavish copying for years and years. I think it is unfortunate that he uses the word *memory* to mean only one aspect of memory. But Blake had an excellent memory, and people with excellent memories are like people with excellent digestions: they're often rather insensitive about their luck.

CAYLEY: How did Blake's views contrast with those of his more conventional contemporaries? What was his relation to his eighteenth-century milieu?

FRYE: Of course, he was almost totally isolated from his eighteenth-century milieu. There were about five or six people who could see what he was about. But the others, he just put all of their anxieties up.

CAYLEY: What does he mean by natural religion? Why did he denounce it in his contemporaries?

FRYE: By natural religion he means the religion we derive from the sense of design in nature. The sense of design in nature is something we've already put there as a mental construct, so we're really staring in the mirror like Narcissus. In other words, we get nothing from passive contemplation of the world. All real knowledge and understanding is creative, that is, it's an activity in man himself, and so all religion is revealed by the imagination to man. But you don't get any religion from contemplating nature, or at least what you do is to invent gods in the image of nature and that gives you storm gods and war gods and all the beings who reflect all the stupid things that human beings do. Natural religion was for Blake what the Bible calls idolatry. It meant finding something numinous in nature, in the physical environment. The Bible says that there are no gods in nature, that nature is a fellow creature of man, and that while one should love nature, you actually get your spiritual vision through human society. Then you see nature as it is. But all the gods that people have pretended to find in nature are in fact devils. That is, they're projections of the wrong side of man's natural origin. So he hated natural religion because he saw it as turning into what in his day was the Napoleonic War and what he called Druidism, which was something projected on the past that was actually a prophecy of the future, that is, totalitarianism.

CAYLEY: You mention in one of your essays that Blake played the role of spiritual preceptor for you, and I think you recommend to other critics that they develop such a relationship with a particular poet.[122] What has been your continuing relationship with Blake?

FRYE: I was originally attracted to him because he made sense of the background I was brought up in. He continued to make that kind of sense for me in the developments I've made in the synoptic theory of criticism in the *Anatomy* and in my later interest in the Bible. Blake, again, was the person who led me to see the shape in the Bible and the reason why it's so central in our cultural tradition.

CAYLEY: You suggest in the passage I'm thinking of that you've also arranged your life in imitation of him.

FRYE: I think that there is a reality in ancestor worship. Let's put it that way. And a person whose role model is Blake is going to be a somewhat different person from a man whose role model is Byron or D. H. Lawrence.

CAYLEY: Did you ever have serious differences with Blake?

FRYE: I think that Blake was perhaps certain of a lot of things I am much less certain of. But that may have been partly his social isolation, where, for reasons of security, he was given to dogmatic assertions. I can't buy his view, for example, that Michelangelo and Raphael are what painting is all about and that Reubens is an incompetent bungler. I can't take that.

CAYLEY: So when you spoke of the tone of mock paranoia in Blake, that was your way of allowing him his eccentricity, of seeing that this is what happens to a supremely sane man in almost intolerable circumstances?

FRYE: Yes, I think that that's true, although I wouldn't say that it was quite the same thing as the mock paranoia. I think that Blake quite deliberately throws himself into a kind of lunatic guise at various times. We're told, by what biographical evidence we have, that he used to do that with people too.

CAYLEY: Sharing so many of your views with Blake, you must have been a bit of a heretic at Emmanuel College?

FRYE: I suppose I was, yes. A lot of my contemporaries regarded me as somebody who just stood outside what they were standing for altogether. My close friends didn't: they knew me better than that. Certainly the dominating ethos then at Emmanuel was Presbyterian and doctrinal in a way that I wasn't. On the other hand, when *Fearful Symmetry* came out in 1947, a professor at Emmanuel said, "How did you manage to do all this reading in contemporary Protestant theology?"

CAYLEY: Meaning?

FRYE: Meaning there had been a tremendous upheaval in Protestant circles, what with Barth and Bultmann and other theologians, since I had been a student at Emmanuel. That was a period of about twelve years.

CAYLEY: And you're saying that you hadn't read these people at all, that you just followed Blake?

FRYE: That's right.

CAYLEY: What else were you reading during your years as a student? What else was truly significant for you or gave you a key piece of the structure you were building?

FRYE: At Hart House library, when I was an undergraduate, I picked up Spengler's *Decline of the West* and was absolutely enraptured with it, and ever since I've been wondering why, because Spengler had one of these muzzy, right-wing, Teutonic, folkish minds. He was the most stupid bastard I ever picked up. But nevertheless, I found his book an inspired book, and finally I've more or less figured out, I think, what I got from Spengler. There's a remark in Malraux's *Voices of Silence* to the effect that he thought that Spengler's book started out as a meditation on the destiny of art forms and then expanded from there. And what it expanded into is the key idea that has always been on my mind, the idea of interpenetration, which I later found in Whitehead's *Science and the Modern World*, the notion that things don't get reconciled, but everything is everywhere at once. Wherever you are is the center of everything. And Spengler showed how that operated in history, so I threw out the muzzy Teuton and kept those two intuitions, which I felt were going to be very central. The other book that enraptured me was Frazer's *Golden Bough*, which, again, was written by a rather stupid man. I felt that scholars could attack this book on practically every ground, but mythically it was the great pyramid, it was solid.

CAYLEY: What about the seasonal metaphor that structures *The Decline of the West*? This also seems to have come into your work.

FRYE: Yes, Spengler has seasonal metaphors, but he doesn't regard history cyclically. He thinks of history as cultures that grow up like dandelions. When the West is declining, the Russian culture starts. But the Russian one was being strangled by Western influence. So the Soviet Union hailed the first volume of *The Decline of the West* with great admiration and damned the second volume, which was on the strangling of Russia under communism. I think that the seasonal metaphors are ones that I adopted more for mnemonic purposes than anything else. I never thought that people would take them so seriously or be so outraged because I reversed the spring and summer ones between an article and a book.

CAYLEY: This idea of your structure-building as a mnemonic device is interesting to me. Had you read Frances Yates's *The Art of Memory*?

FRYE: Yes, but that was published much later.

CAYLEY: Did you already practice an art of memory?

FRYE: I did, but I didn't know it. I'd heard of memory theaters but not enough to know anything at all about them.

CAYLEY: You just made your own?

FRYE: Yes, I just unconsciously acquired my own and had no idea about how you operated with memory theaters until Frances Yates's book came out, which was some time in the mid-sixties.

CAYLEY: So that was all just good luck or instinct?

FRYE: Yes.

CAYLEY: But it was essentially the idea of a structure to which things could then adhere?

FRYE: Yes. I recently gave a paper to an institute concerned with computing in the humanities in which I said that when I wrote the *Anatomy* phrases like "software programming" were entirely unknown. But if they had been known, I think I would have talked more about that and less about my approach being scientific. That bothered a lot of people too.

CAYLEY: But I don't see why the one way of speaking could have effectively replaced the other.

FRYE: It would be an explanation of the way in which I set up the model. I set up the model not because I thought it was mine, or at least I didn't think I set it up because it was mine. I thought I was setting it up because it was there: my literary experience told me it was there. I don't think I have a psychological compulsion to build models. Rather, there has to be something to supplement the experience of literature. If you like, mine was a construction to end all deconstruction. It was the supplement to end supplements.

CAYLEY: Why do you need that supplement?

FRYE: That's the term the Derrida people use when they are reading a text and deciding that what the author really had on his mind was something different from what he says. That becomes the supplement, which means both something extra and something which completes. I think that the real supplement, the one that lurks behind everything, is a mythical structure which repeats itself.

CAYLEY: And it's a supplement to end all supplements because it's permanent and repeating?

FRYE: Yes.

CAYLEY: Frazer and Spengler, recognizing all their liabilities, were the two people who gave you the key pieces then. They were not the ones you admired, but the ones who gave you something you could borrow or use?

FRYE: Yes, that's right. It was, again, a matter of looking for what I could use, but not for something to believe in.

CAYLEY: What about Whitehead and the idea of interpenetration?

FRYE: The conception of interpenetration, as I said, I found in Whitehead's *Science and the Modern World*. Other people have found it in Mahayana Buddhism and the Avatamsaka sutra. It's a way of accounting for the fact that the center is everywhere. Traditionally we've always defined God as a being whose center is everywhere and whose circumference is nowhere. But I would think of God as a being whose center is everywhere and whose circumference is everywhere too. The opposite of interpenetration, where everything exists everywhere at once, is an objective centrality, which, it seems to me, is a most tyrannical conception.

CAYLEY: Objective centrality — what does that mean?

FRYE: In political developments, for example, it's a matter of an empire getting so big that everything gets centered on Rome or London or New York or Tokyo. That seems to me an anticultural direction. In an interpenetrating world every community would be the center of the world.

CAYLEY: What about the social and political thirties in which you came of age? How do you think that entered into your choice of a vocation?

FRYE: When I was compelled to reread *Fearful Symmetry* in order to write a preface to a reprint of it, I discovered what I hadn't realized before: how very troubled a book it was and how much the rise of Nazism was on my mind and how terrified I was by the clarity with which Blake saw things like Druidism coming, whereby human sacrifice, as he says, would have depopulated the earth.

CAYLEY: With your interest in myth and symbol, you entered early on into a kind of magical territory where a lot of people seem to have turned wrong politically. Yeats and Pound and Eliot, in their different ways, would all be examples. But you seem to have always kept your head.

FRYE: Well, it was Blake who helped me to keep my head. One of the books I picked up was Rosenberg's *Myth of the Twentieth Century*, which was a big Nazi polemic claiming that the racially pure come from Atlantis and so forth. Having been concentrating on Blake so heavily, I could see that this was the devil's parody of Blake. I think Yeats plunged into something rather similar without realizing that it was the devil's parody of Blake, although Yeats knew Blake.

CAYLEY: So it was Blake but also your Christianity that kept you sane.

FRYE: I suppose so, yes. And I suppose besides being a student of Blake and a Christian, I'm also a bourgeois liberal. I feel that anybody who isn't one, or at least doesn't want to be one, is still in the trees.

CAYLEY: Was it difficult to decide whether to seek ordination?

FRYE: Yes, it was difficult for me. I consulted a friend whose judgment I had great respect for, Hal Vaughan. He asked me what my difficulty was, and I said that various people, including Herbert Davis, a very civilized man, pointed out that it might be embarrassing later on if I had a professional connection with the Church, and Vaughan said, "Well, isn't that your answer?"

CAYLEY: I don't understand that.

FRYE: It's the business of being a witness.

CAYLEY: You mean if it's embarrassing then you should go ahead?

FRYE: Yes.

CAYLEY: And you did go ahead and ended up as a student pastor in Saskatchewan. That's also part of the Frye saga. Was that just an episode outside your life?

FRYE: Not outside my life, no. But I did realize that the active ministry was not for me, simply because it's an administrative job and I had no consuming interest in administration.

CAYLEY: Can you recall those few months in Saskatchewan?

FRYE: Oh, yes, quite well.

CAYLEY: What do you recall about them?

FRYE: I recall my horse, Katy, who was older than I was and who had a trot that she was very proud of. Whenever Katy broke into a trot you had to stand straight up in the stirrups and let the saddle come up and caress your backside at intervals. I remember something that I found later in a Canadian critic, I think it was Elizabeth Waterson, who spoke of the prairies as the sense of immense space with no privacy. And I found that on top of Katy, who naturally stimulated one's bladder very considerably. I realized that I couldn't get off in that vast stretch of prairie because everybody was out with opera glasses, you see, watching the preacher on top of Katy.

CAYLEY: There must have been some place between the range of the opera glasses. You really were observed to that extent?

FRYE: That was what people did. They all had spy glasses. They weren't doing it with any malicious sense. It was just that their lives were rather devoid of incident, and naturally they liked to see who was going along. It wasn't their fault.

CAYLEY: And the people lived in rather poor circumstances?

FRYE: Oh, yes. The field I was in was a little better off than the ones that were all grasshoppers and dust. They had a kind of subsoil irrigation, which kept them alive, but it was discouraging for them.

CAYLEY: So you were there for just a summer?

FRYE: Yes, a summer. I thought the people were wonderful, but again, I realized that this wasn't the thing I would be good at.

III
ANATOMY OF CRITICISM

CAYLEY: How does *Anatomy of Criticism* connect with your work on Blake? Did you realize at the time *Fearful Symmetry* was published that you had something bigger on your hands?

FRYE: Yes, very quickly I realized that there was another structure there and that a lot of it I had tried to stuff into the Blake book unsuccessfully. It was time to take a look at that independently of Blake.

CAYLEY: You say in the introduction to the *Anatomy* that it forced itself onto you. It sounds as if you were a bit unwilling.

FRYE: In a sense, I was. What I expected to do next was write a book on Spenser, because I was teaching *The Faerie Queene*. Spenser had a great many things in common with Blake, and he was a major influence on Milton, so I settled very happily into collecting notes for a book on Spenser. But in order to get down to Spenser I had to talk about the theory of criticism, and the theory of criticism got longer and longer and more and more elaborate until I finally had to junk Spenser, though he did get into the book. The *Anatomy* came out in bits and pieces — the theory of modes, the circle of myths, and so forth.

CAYLEY: What is an anatomy? Why did you call it that?

FRYE: The word *anatomy* in Shakespeare's day and a little later meant a dissection for a synthetic overview. One of my favorite books in English literature — there are times when it is actually my favorite — is Burton's *Anatomy of Melancholy*. Of course, there were four humors then, but for Burton there was only the one, melancholy. That was the source of all mental and physical diseases in the world. So he writes an enormous survey of human life. It ranks with Chaucer and Dickens, except the characters are books rather than people. It was both an analysis of the causes and cures and treatment of melancholy and a kind of synthetic overview of human nature before it gets melancholy. On a much smaller scale there was Lyly's *Euphues: The Anatomy of Wit*, which has given us the word *euphuism*, meaning that if you're too bright and don't know enough you can get into trouble. That use of the term *anatomy* was one that I thought exactly fitted what I was doing.

CAYLEY: Did you suffer from melancholy yourself?

FRYE: To the extent that I was poor and very much thrown back on myself, yes. But there are two sides to that, the side of alienation and the side of self-reliance. If there's nobody else but yourself, you have to depend on yourself. Burton has a long episode on miseries of scholars, which I certainly reacted to at one time.

CAYLEY: Why is Burton's book sometimes your favorite?

FRYE: Because here was a man writing with tremendous erudition and tremendous exuberance. The fact that he'd referred to about six hundred books per page practically never blotted his sense of humor. He wrote with an almost childlike delight in what he was writing.

CAYLEY: The *Anatomy* begins with a "Polemical Introduction," as you call it. I reread it this summer, and I was struck by its forcefulness and a kind of bracing quality. How did you see the environment into which you were sending this book?

FRYE: I felt that the world of criticism was inhabited by a lot of people who were pretty confused about what they were doing and didn't particularly mind that they were confused. I was also impatient with all the semiliterate productions that I had been compelled to read in the way of secondary sources. I was tired of a historical approach to literature that didn't know any literary history but that simply dealt with ordinary history, adding a few dates of writers. I was tired of people who said that books like *Gulliver's Travels* and *Moby-Dick* were just untidy books, when they should have said they were Menippean satires. It was just a matter of being fed up with a field that seemed to have no discipline in it.

CAYLEY: What's a Menippean satire?

FRYE: It's something that comes down from classical times. There was a Cynic philosopher named Menippus, who wrote a kind of parody of the Platonic dialogue with a certain romance theme. We know the kind of thing he did from Lucian, who picked it up in Greek, and Apuleius, who did it in Latin. That's the kind of tradition that *Gulliver's Travels* belongs to. It's a type of fiction that deals with ideas, usually crank ideas, rather than with people. As I looked at it, it was a subdivision of the anatomy genre itself.

CAYLEY: I believe some of your literary productions as an undergraduate were satires. You were attracted to this form of satire?

FRYE: I was always attracted to that form, because at that time certainly, like most students, I knew more about ideas than I did about people. If somebody like Borges had been known to me at the time, I would have tried to pick up that kind of tradition, I think.

CAYLEY: You also remark in *Fearful Symmetry* that Blake can be better understood sometimes if he is seen as a satirist.

FRYE: One of Blake's earliest works was an extraordinarily funny satire called *An Island in the Moon*, which is a perfect Menippean satire. And I think *The Marriage of Heaven and Hell* is satiric too. What it's satiric of is Milton, Swedenborg and Jehovah, in that order.

CAYLEY: The *Anatomy* is a claim for the autonomy of literary criticism. In what ways did literary criticism lack autonomy at the time that you began writing?

FRYE: By autonomy I mean having a discipline. If you study history, you're a historian, and history has a discipline. There are certain rules for writing correct history, and ways of writing sloppy history that eventually get recognized as such. The same thing is true of philosophy. Criticism, it seemed to me, had no discipline of that kind. It had no sense of its own integrity. I think autonomy was a rather misleading word in some respects, because it suggested to a lot of people who wanted to have this suggested that criticism as I conceived it was a retreat from the world. In fact, the original Italian translator of the *Anatomy* used the word *fuori*, meaning "outside," which was a complete misapprehension of autonomy. The translation has been revised since then. But I didn't think of either criticism or literature as in any respects withdrawing from life. I thought that criticism was a study in its own right and not simply a parasitic approach to literature.

CAYLEY: It's hard for me, certainly in light of your later work, to see that misunderstanding of you as anything but willful on the part of people who have maintained it. But I guess it has been persistent.

FRYE: Oh, yes, especially with left-wing Marxist critics who tend to think that anybody who doesn't take their line is retreating into his bourgeois liberal cave.

CAYLEY: What was criticism subservient to at the time you wrote? That is, what were the forces outside it that dominated it, to which it attached itself?

FRYE: The things I was attacking were the reductive or deterministic criticisms, such as the Marxist, the Freudian, and, at that time, the Thomist type.

CAYLEY: The Thomists were notably at the University of Toronto, I think.

FRYE: Yes.

CAYLEY: You never mentioned any names. But that was at the time of Gilson's great influence.

FRYE: Oh, yes.

CAYLEY: There's also a suggestion that criticism is and should become scientific. You've said that the choice of the term was problematic. Respecting that, what did you mean by speaking that way?

FRYE: By scientific I meant progressive, so that criticism could build on the work of its predecessors in the way that a physicist builds on the work of earlier physicists. There is a metaphor about hard science and soft science, and I've never been impressed by that metaphor. I knew that my conception of science was as soft as a marshmallow, but I didn't give a damn.

CAYLEY: Where would you have located criticism at the time you wrote in terms of the trajectories of other sciences as they developed?

FRYE: Criticism was just lying around in bits and pieces. It wasn't a discipline at all. Therefore, it couldn't be a progressive one.

CAYLEY: So did you see yourself as doing something analogous to what, say, Darwin did for biology, or at least as beginning to give criticism that kind of focus?

FRYE: I hoped that I would, as Francis Bacon says, ring a bell to call the wits together, and that I would awaken some people at any rate to the fact that criticism could be a lot better organized than it had been. But my main strategy was to keep away from the parasitic view of criticism on the one side, and the deterministic one on the other. Criticism neither should be parasitic on literature nor should it be derived from or attached to something that is not literature.

CAYLEY: Had Blake been a preceptor in this regard — in showing you what the critic is or can be?

FRYE: I think I learned everything I knew more or less from Blake. He must have been in the background there somewhere.

CAYLEY: I'm thinking of a remark you made in an essay on Blake, where you say that it was Blake who initially showed you the critic's path by showing that creation and the awareness of that creation are ideally one.[123]

FRYE: Yes. Blake himself said that he had to create a system or be enslaved by another man's.[124] I applied that to criticism generally: one had to see a systematic integrity within criticism or else be taken over by the Marxists, the Freudians, the Thomists, who would then fight among themselves.

CAYLEY: Recognizing again that autonomy may not have been the ideal word, this view that literature has an independent existence, that it constitutes an order of words, by which I think you intend an analogy to an order of nature — does this view provoke anxiety?

FRYE: It seems to, and I've never quite understood why.

CAYLEY: Maybe you can tell me the history of the anxiety then, if you can't explain it.

FRYE: What I always kept getting were anxieties of the kind, "But what about life, Professor Frye?" And

I would say, "But literature is full of life. Life is inside literature. All you have to do to find out about life is just read literature." Oh, my, that bothered them. They were bothered by the suggestion that a writer gets what he acquires technically out of other books instead of by empiric observation. They just had to have it the other way. I began to realize that a great many academics were in fact frustrated poets and novelists, who didn't like the idea of limitations applied to poetry and the novel. If you are interested in writing poetry or a novel and haven't got very far with it, you don't like the idea of there being conventions or genres or limitations of any kind on your capacity. So I used to get all kinds of anxieties about my not attending to the uniqueness of the work of art. And I would keep saying that uniqueness is not an object of knowledge. We never know the unique. The unique exists in experience only. It's part of the response to literature, but it's not part of literature. People still seem to regard that simply as the old art-for-art's-sake paradox of the nineteenth century in a new guise, and that one is running away from all sorts of social responsibilities if one maintains that literature is a structure.

CAYLEY: Were you also provoking anxieties that go all the way back to Plato's banishing the poets from the republic and wanting literature always to be attached to some ideological structure?

FRYE: Well, yes, Plato was the first to want to take over poetry and hitch it onto an ideology, namely his. All the poets who wouldn't do that would have to leave the republic. But according to *The Laws* there are others who stayed around writing hymns and

panegyrics to the greatness of the Platonic idea.
That's still true of all ideologues.

CAYLEY: You've talked about the anxiety provoked
by the idea that literature creates literature, that
most of what the poet is doing is working with
things that have already been done. For the structure
of that world of myth you use the word *archetype* in
the *Anatomy*. What are these archetypes?

FRYE: Archetypes are myths and units within
myths. They are the repeating elements of literature.
They can be anything from conventional images to
story patterns.

CAYLEY: Are they universal? Or are they restricted
to particular cultures?

FRYE: They are culturally conditioned, certainly.
They never transcend the cultural and social environment. But they are universal in the sense that the
Chinese or Japanese drama is recognized by West-
erners as drama, as dramatic experience.

CAYLEY: What is a myth?

FRYE: A myth is a story — the Greek word *mythos*.
It has a beginning, a middle, and an end, whereas
life doesn't.

CAYLEY: How does your use of the term *archetype*
relate to the way, say, Carl Jung uses it?

FRYE: I used the word *archetype* because it was a
traditional term in criticism, though not many people had ever run across it. But I didn't realize at the
time that Jung had monopolized the term and that
everybody would think I was a Jungian critic because I used it. I'm dealing with a world that is
intermediate between the subjective psychological
world and the social world, the objective or natural

world. That is, I don't think in terms of a subject contemplating an object. I think of a world of metaphor, where the subject and object have fused, the world of myth and metaphor. The old-fashioned term for it was *beauty*. It's the world where emotion is relevant, where the categories of beauty and ugliness are relevant, where you don't look for objective truth and you don't look for subjective turmoil. What I don't want to do is to reduce criticism to something subjective and psychological. Jung's archetypes are powers within the soul, and they have very intimate and very fascinating analogies to some of the conventional characters of literature, but Jung's treatment of literature, I think, is barbaric, and most of the Jungians don't seem to be much better.

CAYLEY: He doesn't recognize this intermediate world, in your view?

FRYE: I suppose he would in theory, but after all, his job is the psychological one. That's what he's preoccupied with. To try to make a literary extension of Jung's archetypes would impoverish criticism, in my view, exactly in the same way that Marxist, Freudian, and Thomist criticism impoverished it. I don't want a Jungian criticism. When I was writing the Blake book I deliberately avoided Jung because I didn't want to write a Jungian book on Blake. At that stage I was afraid I would. I read Jung afterwards, and then it was all right.

CAYLEY: Is it possible to find an origin for an archetype, a beginning to a myth?

FRYE: I don't think one can find beginnings, because written literature — the thing we have documents for — goes back to hundreds of thousands of years of oral literature, so that anything like a starting point is lost in the mists of the late Pleistocene.

CAYLEY: So does man make the myths? Or is it rather that the myths make man — in the beginning?

FRYE: It's probably a cooperative enterprise. An astonishing number of people — and some very unlikely people — feel that it's language that uses man rather than man who uses language. And I have a great deal of sympathy for that feeling. It's partly because central to my whole thinking is "In the beginning was the Word."

CAYLEY: So that would argue that the myths are latent in language from the beginning?

FRYE: Yes. I think the primitive impulse in the use of words, the use of language, is to set up a kind of counter-environment. You can teach a chimpanzee to understand sign language if you've got enough bananas on hand, but he wants the counter-environment set up to express what I call his concerns — things like food and sex and company and property and so forth.

CAYLEY: There's a story in Gregory Bateson's last book, *Mind and Nature*, of a man who wants to inquire of a computer whether the computer thinks that computers will ever be able to think. He types in the question, and the computer answers, "That reminds me of a story." That's similar to what you're saying, in a way. I think Bateson's point is that story is ultimate. You can't look behind it and ask what was there before the story. You can't ask whether we made the story or the story made us.

FRYE: According to the poets themselves, there was nothing. Faust is told by Mephistopheles he has to go down to the world of the mothers, but this is the world of nothingness, and what he fishes up are the stories that go into the second part of *Faust*.

CAYLEY: Could you give an example of the structure you see in the sequence of modes that occur in the history of literature? What are the modes?

FRYE: If you're going to tell a story, you're going to have to have characters. They're the most important units of a story. Stories differ from the point of view of the size of the characters and the reader's attitude toward them. Traditionally, say around Homer's time, the central character of a story was a hero, that is, a man who was more than life-size. In the still earlier stories, some of which are incorporated into Homer, there are gods. So you can see that there's a descending series of characters. There's a god, first of all, the biggest one you can imagine. Then there's the hero, who is human but more than life-size. Then there's the leader, the titanic figure like King Lear or Othello or Hamlet, who is, again, recognizably human but conforms to the general operations of nature. Then there's the person like yourself. In that kind of mode, which we find in the Romantic movement, the poetic hero is generally the poet himself, and in fiction, he is a character more or less on our level. Finally, in the ironic mode, the characters are below us; they are in a position of greater frustration or absurdity than we are. It doesn't mean you take a smug view. It's simply a matter of perspective.

CAYLEY: Do the modes form a line? Or is it a circle?

FRYE: It's a circle, because irony goes back again to myth.

CAYLEY: How does irony reach the gods?

FRYE: Eventually you begin to realize that when you have irony you know more about what's going on than the characters do. So you gradually acquire the feeling that there's another half to the whole business of irony. Irony appeals to a sense of what is normal in the audience. Eventually irony goes into reverse, in a sense; it relates itself to what makes a situation ironic. So you go back to myth and romance. When I wrote the *Anatomy*, science fiction was not yet in the center of popular literature, but I knew that it would be very soon, because it would revive Romantic and eventually mythical formulas.

CAYLEY: And in five years we were all poring over Tolkien. Can you give an example of a work in which you can see a myth beginning to peer out from behind irony?

FRYE: Well, one example would be some of the later stories of Henry James, who learned his trade from the ironic novelists of the nineteenth century and whose stories usually end ironically. As he goes on, you find this curious occult streak in him — in stories like "The Altar of the Dead" or "The Sense of the Past" or "The Turn of the Screw," where the irony in seeing the absurdity and frustration of a human situation begins to suggest the gods' point of view. The God of the Book of Job must have taken a very similar view of the human situation.

CAYLEY: Another of your ideas in the Anatomy is that myths go through a series of displacements. That's a term that you borrowed from psychoanalysis.

FRYE: Yes. Freud says that two operations of the dream are condensation and displacement. I think there is condensation and displacement in literature as well, though it operates very differently, of course. You have displacement when you have a structure made credible or plausible or lined up with something the reader finds credible. You have condensation when you go the other way, when the structure is intensely metaphorical and has no specific relationship to the outside world. The most condensed book ever written was *Finnegans Wake*. You get displacement in its most extreme when you get a totalitarian government insisting that everybody write allegories of their own fantasies.

CAYLEY: What would be an example from literature of displacement?

FRYE: The naturalistic novel. A book like Truman Capote's *In Cold Blood* would go even further.

CAYLEY: Where there is an almost subliminal mythic structure . . .

FRYE: There has to be a story with a beginning, a middle, and an end. Wherever there is a story with a beginning, a middle, and an end, there is always a myth, because that's what myth means — story. In an intensely displaced structure, the story line is still there but the main emphasis is focused on its similarity to experience.

CAYLEY: The other thing from the *Anatomy* which became notorious and caused you to write several clarifications was your position on value judgments, your refusal to think of the critic as primarily a taste-maker. What were you getting at there, and what were the consequences of your trying to get at it?

FRYE: I was getting at the conception of the critic as judge, as sitting on a bench with the defendant in front of him squirming. I felt that that was a preposterous ego trip for the critic to attempt. Value judgments are things that people argue about and discuss endlessly, and they do enter into one's critical experience. The thing is that they can never be demonstrated. What a value judgment manifests is the taste of its time, and it's filtered through the individual critic. The value judgment of the most serious critics for a century after Shakespeare's death was that Ben Jonson was really a much more serious writer. Value judgments of the later eighteenth century said that Blake was a lunatic. The great boners of criticism, such as Rymer's calling *Othello* a bloody farce, are not the result of a critic's lack of taste.[125] They're the result of his following the conventions of his time.

CAYLEY: Did you feel that was the dominant self-image of critics at the time?

FRYE: In the eighteenth century there was a great deal of feeling that, as Samuel Johnson says, "The drama's laws, the drama's patrons give, / For we that live to please, must please to live."[126] Well, that is true, but with other people, like Addison, for example, you get public taste set up as the arbiter of literary quality.

CAYLEY: What is the alternative view?

FRYE: The alternative view is that value judgments have to be under veto by the changes in the history of taste. Every age is inadequate in its taste. As the age changes, its canons of taste will change too. Every positive change rescuing a neglected writer is good.

CAYLEY: Why do you think there was such misunderstanding on this point?

FRYE: There was great misunderstanding because people were brought up to think that being a literary critic was a gentleman's occupation, and the gentleman is the person who attaches immense importance to his taste: I like this, I don't like that.

CAYLEY: In rejecting that, where were you trying to go as a critic?

FRYE: In rejecting that, you move from the gentleman to the scholar. The scholar reads everything in his historical period. It's all good, because it's all documentation for his work. He works entirely without explicit value judgments. They may enter into his work at some point or other, but good, bad, or indifferent, everything that comes under the literary scholar's purview has to be read by the scholar.

CAYLEY: He's trying to understand, not to judge?

FRYE: Yes, and very often you can understand the taste of an age from its least interesting writers.

CAYLEY: In rejecting criticism as a gentleman's occupation, you're also implicitly trying to democratize criticism.

FRYE: To democratize criticism and also to remove criticism from the area of morality, because every value judgment is a moral judgment in disguise.

CAYLEY: What are the consequences of doing that?

FRYE: The moral judgment reflects the ideological conditioning of a certain age. Every age is mortal.

I'm not trying to eliminate value judgments from the critical practice; I'm merely pointing out their grave limitations and the fact that so many judgments have been thought of as transcending the age in which they're made. Of course, they never do.

CAYLEY: Presumably you couldn't eliminate them if you wanted to.

FRYE: You can't eliminate them.

CAYLEY: You're just showing them as something limited, conditioned, and not at the center of activity?

FRYE: Yes. The nearest you come to a value judgment, I think, are in words like *classic* or *masterpiece*, where you have value terms, but what they mean are works of literature that refuse to go away. It was all very well to say for a century that Ben Jonson was a closer follower of nature than Shakespeare and therefore a far more serious dramatist, but Shakespeare just squatted down on the stage and refused to move and survived even the most grotesque manhandlings of his work, whereas only two or three of Jonson's plays have really held the stage.

CAYLEY: So now if one says that Shakespeare is a great writer one is doing something other than making a value judgment?

FRYE: Yes, and you also find in the course of your critical experience that some writers are more rewarding to deal with than others. You find that confirmed by your experience. I'm not suggesting that criticism can ever be a value-free thing; I'm merely trying to take out the tyranny of value judgments from the critical enterprise.

CAYLEY: Your *Anatomy* begins with a "Polemical

Introduction" and ends with only a "Tentative Conclusion" but nevertheless expresses a hope for criticism. I notice in a later book you remark that many critics are still mired in ideology. How do you see your project for criticism with more than thirty years of hindsight?

FRYE: I see it partly as a matter of distinguishing between ideology and poetics. I think that the ideologue addresses the public and wants to make a kinetic effect on them. He wants them to get out there and do something. The poet turns his back on his audience. I begin the *Anatomy* with John Stuart Mill's remark that the poet is overheard, not heard, and he doesn't look for a kinetic effect on his audience at all. He's creating an absence so that his audience can move into a presence.

CAYLEY: But the *Anatomy* was a manifesto for a scientific or disinterested criticism. In your view, has that come into existence?

FRYE: No, it hasn't, partly because of the very nature of language as it's used by critics, particularly humanist critics. That is, it's a matter of where you put your emphasis, and where you put your emphasis can never be definitively right or wrong. I still think that there is an underlying consensus of agreement among the really top-flight critics — the people who obviously know what they're talking about. But they themselves wouldn't care to admit that.

CAYLEY: What do you mean?

FRYE: I mean that you pick up an academic article, and after the first sentence there's a footnote, and the footnote refers you to twenty-seven previous articles on the same subject. If you check up on the twenty-seven articles, you'll find that about four of them are written by people who know what they're saying. The others are doing literary exercises demonstrating their competence in handling criticism, but not contributing to its knowledge.

CAYLEY: I'm still not sure you've answered my question about whether you see progress along the line you sketched out in the *Anatomy*.

FRYE: I think I see, as I say, a kind of implicit consensus, which means that there is also a kind of implicit progress. There are certain kinds of critical junk that are definitely obsolete. We don't have to bother with them very much now. There are an awful lot of new kinds, and we have to get rid of them too.

CAYLEY: You mention in another essay that if you want to make a splash you should make it at a time when a path of knowledge is forking, when a change is about to take place, when one discipline is about to precipitate out of another, and you use the example of Freud. You say that if Freud had written today, he probably would have been regarded as a crank with insufficient clinical experience.

FRYE: I wrote that at a time when all psychologists were chasing rats and wouldn't have anything to do with human beings.

CAYLEY: Do you think you found such a moment with the *Anatomy*?

FRYE: I would have to write a very different book today, because I would have to deal with the developments of criticism since 1957. That would mean that I would have to consider all kinds of things that didn't come into the *Anatomy* because they weren't around in 1957.

CAYLEY: I was thinking rather of the fact that within ten years of the *Anatomy*'s coming out it was, in a sense, the book to be reckoned with. Was that because of the opportune moment at which you published it?

FRYE: I daresay, yes.

CAYLEY: Did it then become something of an albatross for you?

FRYE: To the extent that it's been so persistently and, it seems to me, often deliberately misunderstood, it has become something of an albatross. So much so that I confessed to a very good friend in a letter that I rather regretted having written it. But of course I don't really.

CAYLEY: All of that misunderstanding surely stimulated you to produce other books.

FRYE: Well, yes.

CAYLEY: When you wrote the *Anatomy of Criticism*, you'd written one book on Blake. When did you realize that you had written not just another book but what was being described within ten years as the book of its generation? When did you begin to realize what the *Anatomy* was going to mean to people?

FRYE: I thought it would clarify things and perhaps set criticism going in a more systematic and progressive direction. It didn't do what I had hoped it would do, but then it was naive to hope that. You have to have certain illusions in front of your nose if you're writing, and when you've finished writing you don't mind if they fade away.

CAYLEY: I remember at the memorial service for C. B. Macpherson you recalled a time in both of your youths when you could meet for coffee as friends and not, you said, as a collision of monuments. When did you begin to feel that you'd become a monument?

FRYE: It's something that comes gradually with age. It's not so much the hardening of the arteries as a hardening of what some people call the character-ological armor.

CAYLEY: But in saying that you seem to blame yourself. I understood your joke about you and Brough Macpherson to refer more to the embarrassment of reputation than to anything that had actually happened to you.

FRYE: It's a reciprocal thing. It's something that other people do to you, and you have to react to it somehow.

IV
CRITICAL ARGUMENTS

CAYLEY: I'd like to ask you about your critics. The ones
I have read all seem to be saying that you think of
myth as immaculately conceived. A psychoanalytic
critic, like Frederick Crews, says that you're concealing the origin of myth in discontent.[127] A Marxist
critic, like Frederic Jameson, says that you've erased
the mark of ideology from myth.[128] And even Geof-
frey Hartman says at one point — in *Northrop Frye
and Modern Criticism* — that myth comes to us already institutionalized: we never see it in any other
way.[129] So all three, it seems to me, are finally saying
the same thing, that you have a version of myth as
pure, as archetypal, as free from its social origins,
and distinguishable from the institutionalized

forms in which it appears to us. How do you see this criticism?

FRYE: Let's start with the statement that myth comes to us already institutionalized. Now there are some myths that do come to us institutionalized. Those are the ideological myths, the myths that underlie official Christianity or the Church or institutionalized Judaism, Islam, Marxism, and so forth. But most of my critics do not know that there is such a thing as a poetic language, which not only is different from ideological language but puts up a constant fight against it to liberalize and individualize it. There is no such thing as a pure myth. There's no immaculate conception of mythology. Myth exists only in incarnations. But it's the ones that are incarnated in works of literature that I'm primarily interested in, and what they create is a cultural counter-environment to the ones that are — I won't say perverted — but at any rate twisted or skewed into ideological patterns of authority.

CAYLEY: I think that critics like Jameson are saying that all myths are in some sense skewed.

FRYE: They say that because they are pan-ideologists. They can't conceive of any myth that doesn't come in an ideological form. But for Shakespeare myth is not ideological. Dante and Milton perhaps more obviously reflect the ideology of their time, but their structure is radically a poetic structure, which is something different.

CAYLEY: So you're saying that all these critics, in their different ways, don't finally accept the claim for the autonomy of poetry that you have made throughout your life?

FRYE: Yes, that's right.

CAYLEY: And that's why you've said repeatedly there's really not enough in common between you and these people to have a discussion?

FRYE: Yes.

CAYLEY: Have you ever entered into dialogue with any of your critics on this issue?

FRYE: No. I detest arguments. You're going to lose any argument with an ideologue, because you can only argue on the basis of a counter-ideology, and I'm not doing that.

CAYLEY: Are there critics you've learned from, critics with whom you've shared enough in common that they could teach you something?

FRYE: There are critics, yes, who know what I'm talking about.

CAYLEY: But no case in which you've really seen something as a result of criticism of your work?

FRYE: Well, I'm afraid I learn very little from my critics. That's not arrogance. It's just self-preservation.

CAYLEY: It seems to me you've run in parallel with various contemporary intellectual trends without exactly being part of them. The *Anatomy*, for example, seems to embody elements of what was called structuralism.

FRYE: I stumble into things. When I published *Fearful Symmetry* I was told on all sides, by all my reviewers, that I was a myth critic. At that point I didn't know what the hell a myth critic was, and I certainly didn't realize that there was a school called myth criticism. But I did know that you had to know something about myth to understand or to expound

Blake. Similarly, when the *Anatomy* came out I had no idea what structuralism was — I'd never heard the word — but I did know that literature had a structure, and I tried to give some impression of what it was.

CAYLEY: When you found out what it was, what did you think of it as an approach?

FRYE: Again, the structuralists seem to be interested in other things — in linguistic and semiotic applications — which I had no direct interest in. I was naturally very interested in Lévi-Strauss and his parallels between poetic structures and, say, kinship structures in anthropology, but that's not a field where I can follow him at all.

CAYLEY: But all of this still would come under your strictures about the search for a giant lever to move the world of literature, rather than working from within the world of literature?

FRYE: Yes, I think so. Structuralism tried to straddle a whole field of language. As a result it ran into a poststructural ideology, and that's something I cannot relate to somehow.

CAYLEY: How do you mean?

FRYE: Well, the little book of Jean Piaget on structuralism stretches all over language and all over mathematics as well. I can't stretch that far. I'm concerned only with works of literature and distinguishing poetic structures from others, including ideological ones.

CAYLEY: Jacques Derrida is someone who seems to have had an immense influence in literary criticism.

FRYE: Derrida seems to have continued the whole tradition of the analytic, rhetorical criticism I encountered when I started the *Anatomy*. He's put it on a more philosophical basis with his conception of a logic of supplement. As a result, he's developed a group of disciples who don't accept anything as an authentic text except what Derrida has written and has scratched out again. I think that that's an interesting technique in many respects, but I think it's also exhaustible.

CAYLEY: What is a logic of supplement?

FRYE: A logic of supplement means that what actually appears in a text is always written for a more complex mind. Consequently, there are many things in your mind that have been suppressed from the text, and the criticism of supplement attempts to indicate what some of those are.

CAYLEY: That's deconstruction?

FRYE: That's deconstruction, yes. Rousseau wrote on the origin of language, but he was primarily interested in masturbation, so your criticism says that.

CAYLEY: This is obviously not an approach you would find congenial.

FRYE: No. Well, I can see the point of it. But it is not something that I either know how to do or want to do.

CAYLEY: So the critical schools that have succeeded each other in your time have really defeated your hope for a unified and progressive science of criticism in the *Anatomy*?

FRYE: They would have if they were winning.

CAYLEY: But they aren't?

FRYE: I am often described as somebody who is now in the past and whose reputation has collapsed. But I don't think I'm any further down skid row than the deconstructionists are.

CAYLEY: I'm interested in your unwillingness to argue. This ties in with your style of writing. It seems to me that in your books you don't generally present an argument. For a long time I wanted to be able to say, finally, "This is the program that Northrop Frye is arguing for." But I'm not sure any more that that kind of statement is possible.

FRYE: I think that there are implied arguments in what I say, but the actual technique of argumentative writing is something I avoid as far as possible, because when you argue you are selecting points to emphasize, and there can never be anything definitively right or wrong about an emphasis. It's simply a choice among possibilities. Consequently, an argument is always a half-truth. We've known that ever since Hegel. It is a militant way of writing, and I'm not interested in militancy. As I've often said, the irrefutable philosopher is not the person who cannot be refuted but the philosopher who's still there after he's been refuted.

CAYLEY: What's the alternative to argument?

FRYE: Literature doesn't argue. That's the principle of Shelley's *Defence of Poetry* — that literature cannot argue. As Yeats says, "You can refute Hegel but not the Song of Sixpence." The whole argumentative side is something that critics, without examining the matter, think must be true of criticism if not of literature. But to me criticism is really the expression of the awareness of language. And what I try to do in my writing is express awareness of language, particularly of literary language and what it's trying to do.

CAYLEY: In your latest book, *Words with Power*, you

have an interesting quotation from Bertrand Russell. He says, "Each philosopher, in addition to the formal system which he offers to the world, has another much simpler of which he may be quite unaware. If he is aware of it, he realizes it probably won't quite do. He therefore conceals it and sets forth something much more sophisticated which he believes, because it is like his crude system, but which he asks others to accept because he thinks he has made it such as it cannot be disproved." Is there a crude system of this sort behind your writings?

FRYE: What Bertrand Russell is saying could be considered under two metaphors. One is that the myth is the naked body and that the philosophical structure is the clothes that make it possible for the body to appear in society. The other is that the philosophy is the body and the myth is the skeleton underneath the body. You can take either of those metaphors, but they both say that there is something that cannot go around on its own without this philosophical superstructure, or whatever it is. There have been a few naked systems, like Yeats's *Vision* and Poe's *Eureka* and, to some extent, Dante's *Convivio*, which he offers partly as an explanation of what the cosmology of his poetry is about. I think that that is something that is worth looking into. Paul Valéry, commenting on Poe's *Eureka*, says that cosmology is really at bottom a literary structure.

CAYLEY: When I read the Russell quotation, it made me feel that there is in all your writing a simpler structure, a basic myth that is being elaborated or dressed up.

FRYE: I don't know, though I suppose it could be

the myth of creation — a sense of a total verbal order. I've talked about the verbal universe ever since I've been writing. The idea that the human consciousness lives inside a universe of words, which is in turn inside the universe of nature, has always been very central to me. Of course the difficulty with the word *universe* is that it suggests something spatial, whereas the true verbal universe is a conflict of powers and, consequently, exists in time as well as space.

CAYLEY: It seems to me there's a sense in your writing, very palpable at times, of the possibility of redemption.

FRYE: That's right. Man's destiny is not predetermined. It's his heritage, it's his birthright, it's something he can fulfill if he wants to. So far he hasn't wanted to.

V
MILTON AND THE
ROMANTIC TRADITION

CAYLEY: You've always emphasized the cosmological dimension in poetry, and I'd like to talk about Milton and the Romantic revolution in that light. Was Milton important for you fairly early on in your career?

FRYE: I read him dutifully as an undergraduate and passed examinations on him, but I think I didn't really get into him in any sort of existential depth until I started teaching him. Then I began to see the integrity of the man, the way he holds together: the political polemicist and the baroque poet and all the other sides of him fitted together so admirably. He is obviously a person of towering stature. If you teach Milton, you find that those tremendous lines in *Paradise Lost* begin to separate from their context and take on an individual life and start chasing themselves around your skull. Any poet who does that to you is obviously somebody you have to reckon with.

CAYLEY: I see Milton as being more of a polestar for you than other writers to whom you've devoted equal attention and who would be equally great in your view, Shakespeare or Spenser. Is that true?

FRYE: Perhaps so.

CAYLEY: You're in his lineage?

FRYE: Yes, Milton is solidly within my tradition. He was solidly within Blake's tradition. The combination of the humanist conservative and the revolutionary was a very fascinating one for me.

CAYLEY: How was Milton a revolutionary?

FRYE: He was a revolutionary in the sense that he went through four English revolutions and took the revolutionary side every time, until he was finally checkmated by the Restoration. He fought for liberty all his life, for civil and domestic and ecclesiastical liberty. I felt that I was on his side in all three of these areas. But at the same time he was a conservative in that he thought that liberty was a good thing because it was what God wanted for man, but that man could not and did not want liberty for himself. What man wants always is slavery or mastery. That is, he wants mastery first, and if he can't have mastery he'll settle for slavery.

CAYLEY: With that view how can one have the confidence to take the risk of revolution?

FRYE: Because God wants liberty for man. Therefore, he must be on man's side when man is fighting for liberty.

CAYLEY: Can you explain how Milton's revolutionary views grow out of his Christianity, and his reading of the Gospel?

FRYE: He reads Paul saying, "Stand fast in the liberty, wherein Christ has made you free." The freedom here is from the law, in the sense of internalizing the law. The criminal is not free; he just breaks the law. But the person who has internalized the law is no longer a subject of external obligations; he's an integrated person.

CAYLEY: So only a good man can be free?

FRYE: Only a good man can be free, and there is no antithesis between freedom and necessity. If you're playing the piano and exercising your free will about whether you'll play the right notes or the wrong notes, you're not playing worth a damn. You know what you're doing only when what you want to do and what you have to do are exactly the same thing.

CAYLEY: And that, I think, has been important for you as well.

FRYE: Oh, yes.

CAYLEY: Now to take the other side of Milton, what is the source of his conservatism?

FRYE: His conservative view derives from his belief in original sin, which, of course, every serious Christian has to have. But he didn't draw the preposterous inference from original sin that because man is born in sin he ought to be pushed around by people who, by definition, are no better than he is.

CAYLEY: How did Blake deal with Milton?

FRYE: He dealt with Milton as a person inhibited by the sense of an objective God. In *Paradise Lost* Milton still had the old stinker in the sky. *Paradise Lost* to some extent rationalizes the creation as it stands, whereas for Blake the creation was a bungle, and things start with man recreating a ruined universe.

CAYLEY: You're with Blake?

FRYE: Oh, yes.

CAYLEY: But Blake also says that Milton was of the devil's party without knowing it.[130]

FRYE: There he's using angel and devil in a very specific context. The angels are the conservatives and the devils are the radicals.

CAYLEY: What is the order which Milton rationalizes and Blake rejects?

FRYE: The traditional structure is that theologically there are four levels. There is, first of all, the presence of God, which is always associated with metaphors of "up there," even though they're known to be nothing but metaphors. Then there is the state that God intended man to live in, that is, the Garden of Eden, the Golden Age, Paradise. Then there is, third, the fallen world, the world man fell into with the sin of Adam and Eve. Then there is, fourth, the demonic world, the world below the order of nature. On that scheme, there are two levels to the order of nature, the one that God designed and the one that we're living in now. The destiny of man is to climb out of the fallen world as nearly as he can to the state that was originally designed for him. He does this under a structure of authority: the sacraments of religion, the practice of morality, education, and so forth.

CAYLEY: And what role does poetry play when such an order is intact?

FRYE: Poetry begins with two strikes against it because God made the world and made it better than poets can make poems. Sir Thomas Browne says that nature is the art of God, and of course that means that man just sweeps up the shavings, so to speak.[131] The poets didn't take that as seriously as the theologians did, fortunately. But after about 1750 it came to be clearer and clearer that these four levels were the facade of a structure of authority. With the Romantic movement you get this whole cosmology turned upside down.

CAYLEY: Why at that date did it come to be clear?

FRYE: Because of the American, the French, and the Industrial revolutions.

CAYLEY: What about the scientific revolution? What role did that play?

FRYE: That of course knocked out all of the "up there" metaphors. After Newton's time you couldn't regard the stars as a world of quintessence, as all that was left of the unfallen world. That's why in his poetry Blake gives Isaac Newton the job of blowing the last trumpet.

CAYLEY: What was the alternative view that Blake began?

FRYE: Blake says that we live in, if you like, a fallen world, that is, a world of great inequities, of privilege, a world of ferocity. He doesn't have an idealized view of nature like Rousseau. He doesn't believe in the noble savage. Wordsworth says that nature is our teacher, and the Marquis de Sade says that nature justifies your pleasure in inflicting pain on others. Blake would say that there is a lot more evidence for the Marquis de Sade's view of nature than for Wordsworth's. So for Blake what happens is that the child, who is the central figure of the *Songs of Innocence*, is born believing that the world is made for his benefit, that the world makes human sense. He then grows up and discovers that the world isn't like this at all. So what happens to his childlike vision? Blake says it gets driven underground, what we would now call the subconscious. There you have the embryonic mythical shape that is worked on later by people like Schopenhauer, Marx, and Freud.

CAYLEY: Blake sees the child as innocent. You've also described that as seeing the child as civilized. Does that distinguish Blake from Rousseau? Or are different terms being used to say the same thing?

FRYE: Yes, it does distinguish him from Rousseau and brings him much closer to Milton, who also thought of the original state of man as civilized.

CAYLEY: In the traditional structure the movement is from God to man. What is the movement within Blake's cosmos?

FRYE: For Blake, you have to think of God as at the bottom of creation, trying to rebuild it, and as working through man to that effect.

CAYLEY: The four levels are still there?

FRYE: They're still there, but they're upside down. The world "up there" is the world of science fiction, of outer space. It's a symbol of alienation. There's nothing there except infinite resources for killing you. Then below that comes this very unfair world of ordinary experience, where the predators are the aristocrats. Below that is the world of frustrated sexual and social desire, the world of Marx's proletariat, of Freud's repressed consciousness. And

WORLD ORDER

below that again is the creative power of God, which works only through man as a conscious being.

CAYLEY: How does Blake relate to the Romantic movement?

FRYE: I think Blake wraps up the whole Romantic movement inside himself, although nobody else knew it. You can find a good deal of the upside-down universe in all of the other Romantics, most completely, I think, in Shelley, where in a poem like *Prometheus Unbound* everything that's "up there," namely Jupiter, is tyrannical, and everything that's down in caves is liberating.

CAYLEY: But Shelley takes this in a more atheistical direction than Blake does.

FRYE: Shelley doesn't derive primarily from the biblical tradition in the way that Blake does. Blake is always thinking in terms of the biblical revolutions, the Exodus in the Old Testament and the Resurrection in the New Testament.

CAYLEY: In other words, Blake has a given structure of imagery from the Bible that he works with, and that distinguishes him from the other Romantics.

FRYE: It certainly distinguishes his emphasis from Shelley.

CAYLEY: And that would be an advantage in your view? In *The Critical Path* you talk about the status of poetics and humanism in the Augustan age, and you say that by Coleridge's time, despite Coleridge's own efforts, critics had ceased to teach and poets to learn from them an integrated structure of imagery.[132] You suggest that people were casting about, but, of course, Blake wasn't in any sense casting about. He had only to transform the given structure, whereas Shelley was inventing one.

FRYE: I think that that is true. Shelley keeps picking things up from Plato and others. He would argue endlessly with Byron, who was, in a way, a more Christian poet than Shelley. I think Byron, at any rate, could understand the solidity of the biblical tradition, even when it had been transformed into a structure of authority, whereas Shelley kept changing his mind and tinkering with his cosmology. He knew Plato very well, but there's the authoritarian streak in Plato too, which Shelley didn't like.

CAYLEY: Why is the Romantic movement called Romantic? This seems to be a word like *myth* which has opposed meanings. What does the term mean? And why does romance define this period?

FRYE: There's a long and complex history of the words *romance* and *Romanticism*, all of which I read at one time and all of which I've completely forgotten. So I really can't answer the question from any scholarly point of view, but in general the Romantic is, according at any rate to one notable critic, named Ayme, the mode in which there is a heroic figure who can transcend the laws of nature to some degree. That is, the heroes of medieval romance can accomplish things that in fact no human being can do, as Don Quixote points out. In Romanticism, to some extent, that power gets transferred to the poet, a power of transcending ordinary experience through imagination.

CAYLEY: So that the poet's becoming the hero is what makes for Romanticism?

FRYE: Yes.

CAYLEY: And sometimes leads to the substitution of art for religion?

FRYE: Yes, in the sense that it often turns into something prophetic.

CAYLEY: You've described the Romantic inversion of the traditional order of things as the central mythological event of the modern age. How does it set the terms not just for literature but even for politics and philosophy?

FRYE: Well, it throws the emphasis on movements from below upward. Revolutionary philosophies, like those of Marx and of most Freudians, though not altogether Freud himself, do this: they move from below upwards, or at least tend to draw their strength from what is below. The whole set of metaphors whereby everything that is good for man came from above and came down on top of him has been changed to a set of metaphors where everything that is good for man comes from inside him and works upwards toward manifesting itself.

CAYLEY: In one of your essays you use the image of the drunken boat to represent this change.[133]

FRYE: The image of the drunken boat, which comes from Rimbaud, is the image of a sort of Noah's ark containing all the values of civilization floating on top of something very sinister and powerful that threatens it. Whether the ark will stay afloat or not depends on the optimism of the thinker. With Schopenhauer it was the world of idea floating on top of the world of will. With Marx it was the ascendant class floating on top of a bigger and bigger and stronger proletariat. With Freud it was the ego fighting to stay afloat with the libido and id underneath it. With Kierkegaard, it was again the ego, or something like it, floating on top of angst, of dread.

CAYLEY: It's interesting that although the structure is constant one can make a conservative or revolutionary view out of it, or one can make an optimistic or pessimistic philosophy out of it.

FRYE: Oh, yes. One can take the view of Schopenhauer that the world of will is evil but can't be got rid of. Or one can take the view of Nietzsche that this is what we ought to get hold of and use for ourselves.

CAYLEY: In our century there's been an attempt to retrench on this Romantic cosmology, which you argue has not been entirely successful. You say that the conservative response to Romanticism in Eliot and others had the resources only to become post-Romanticism. It couldn't find a third way between Romanticism and reaction. Why?

FRYE: As a structure of metaphors it doesn't really matter. I mean, you can put all the good things "up there" coming down to man in a shower of blessings. Or you can use the inverted framework. Metaphorically it doesn't matter which you do. And you can have people using traditional Dantean cosmologies, as Eliot does, and make convincing poetry out of them. In a sense, that was what Yeats did too. I think that the answer is Jacob's ladder: there are angels ascending and there are angels descending.

CAYLEY: Then one can't have a third structure of imagery, because there isn't one to be invented?

FRYE: That's right, there isn't one. When you've got everything coming from the top down, you've got a structure of authority, and when you've got everything coming from the bottom up you've got another structure of authority, a revolutionary one. The thing to do is try to duck out from under all structures of authority.

CAYLEY: So when you say that the modern reaction couldn't become anything but a post-Romanticism, you're saying that it could only revert to the earlier structure. If it rejected the Romantic structure, it had no other possibility than reaction.

FRYE: Mythically and metaphorically, as I say, it doesn't matter, but ideologically it's very apt to take on the coloring of the old authority structures.

CAYLEY: You encountered these authority structures particularly in Eliot, about whom you wrote a book, which was not well received by him, I gather.

FRYE: Yes, I did find them in Eliot, though I didn't find fascism in his work. There's flirtation with fascism in Pound and Yeats and others because, again, they were looking back to the earlier metaphorical structure and therefore took on some of its ideological coloring. Eliot didn't go that far, but he was certainly, in my terms, a reactionary. When I read *After Strange Gods* after it first came out, I felt it was a betrayal.

CAYLEY: Was that important for you?

FRYE: It was. In a way it was my becoming aware of my own responsibilities as a critic. Because you couldn't trust the poets, you had to do it yourself if you were going to be a critic.

CAYLEY: So that was the beginning of your understanding that the characters and political views of poets are unrelated to their poetic abilities.

FRYE: Yes. One of my guiding principles is that a poet can be any kind of damn fool and still be a poet.

CAYLEY: How did the Eliot book come about?

FRYE: A firm called Oliver and Boyd of Edinburgh was doing a series on modern poets and they asked me to do Eliot. I was to do a book 192 pages long. I did one that was 216 pages long, and they said that an extra gathering would turn their profit into a loss. So I cut so much out of it that I produced a book of 85 pages, and they didn't quite know what to do with that. Then I had to expand the bloody thing until I got it into 192 pages. It was also a part of the format of the series that you should begin with a biography. So I had to put in a biographical preface, and that was what Eliot himself objected to. I didn't want to write the biography at all, but I did want to write the rest of it. I thought it would be interesting to see if I could get the whole of Eliot into 192 pages. I didn't want to write a biographical sketch, because I didn't think Eliot's biography was relevant to his poetry. I disliked his personality anyway. There just wasn't anything I wanted to say, or anything fresh I had to say, about his life. That rather spoiled the book in some respects, but the rest of it I think was all right.

The first two chapters of the book were on two aspects of his criticism. The first was the ideological and polemical side. I wrote that because I wanted to see whether you could take all of the reactionary element in Eliot and just snip it off with a pair of scissors and leave him intact as a man of letters. And it worked. The thing about Eliot that holds everyone's interest is his extraordinarily memorable quality. He seems to have that knack that Coleridge had in "Kubla Khan" and the "Ancient Mariner" of going just below the surface of consciousness, just far enough to bring up all that haunting power and all the richness and portentousness of the subconscious that is very close to consciousness. And, as I said in the book, you may like or dislike his poetry but you can't forget it once you've read it.

CAYLEY: Yes, I find it amazing how much of Eliot I've retained. Another poet about whom you've written a good deal is Wallace Stevens. Was he someone who challenged you in some way?

FRYE: When I was sixteen working in the Moncton public library, I used to pore over Untermeyer's anthologies of modern American poets, and all there was of Stevens at that time was *Harmonium*, but that fascinated me. That had some of the same qualities that Eliot had, even though it was a very different kind of poetry. I found that Stevens was somebody who held up, whereas so many of the others, like the imagists, just dropped out of my sight. I didn't cease to read them for pleasure, but Wallace Stevens remained something very central. Once the *Collected Poems* came out, I decided I had to write an essay on Stevens.

CAYLEY: Was that "The Realistic Oriole"?[134]

FRYE: Yes. I find myself quoting Stevens very frequently, so frequently that when *The Great Code* came out, the people who interviewed me by telephone from Sydney, Australia, wanted to know why the hell I'd put so much Wallace Stevens in, and I couldn't tell them why, except that he just seemed to fit what I had to say.[135]

CAYLEY: The reason I asked whether he challenged you was because it seems to me that some of those famous phrases you quote from Stevens — "the weight of primary noon," "the dominant X," "one confides in what has no concealed creator" — have a sense of the independent existence of nature and the sense of the imperialism of the imagination and the necessity of there being a struggle with no winner. It seemed to me that this might have challenged your sense of nature's finally being taken inside the enlightened imagination.

FRYE: Well, it was taken inside in him too. "Description without Place" tells you you don't live in a natural environment at all. You live in coating, the husk of human culture or civilization, and you take nature in through that.

CAYLEY: So there's nothing in Stevens that necessarily challenged your own view, although it may have extended it or given it a language?

FRYE: It extended it, yes. It didn't set up anything I couldn't very easily come to terms with.

CAYLEY: I think of Stevens as an atheist.

FRYE: I think of Stevens as a Protestant. I know he turned Catholic on his death bed, but people do funny things on their death beds.

CAYLEY: A nature with "no concealed creator," the earth as "all of paradise that we shall know," the idea of "a supreme fiction" — I suppose that as a young man reading Stevens lines like these suggested atheism to me.

FRYE: He says "in the new world all men are priests," and I think that he had a sense of man assigned to recreate the universe, just as Blake had.

His attitude toward God was very like Emily Dickinson's, who didn't want to repudiate her faith but wanted to fight with it.

CAYLEY: What about the view of nature as uncreated?

FRYE: I think he disliked the thought of God as an artist, because again that writes off the human artist.

CAYLEY: I know nothing about Stevens personally except that he worked in insurance, and obviously my knowledge of his poetry is sketchy too. Was he in fact a religious man in his own way?

FRYE: Oh, I think so, yes. Look at what he says about Easter in "Adagia" in *Opus Posthumous*. He doesn't very often commit himself to a religious statement, but it's there, all right.

VI
THE CRITICAL PATH

CAYLEY: Could we talk now about your book *The Critical Path*, which you wrote around 1970? Perhaps we could begin with the title. Where did that come from?

FRYE: I picked it up as a term in business administration. It set up an echo in my mind of the last paragraph in the *Critique of Pure Reason*, where Kant says we've tried the dogmatic way and it doesn't work, we've tried the skeptical way and it doesn't work; the critical path is alone open. The dogmatist says, "I know that," and the skeptic says, "I don't know that," and the critic tries to figure out what he tentatively knows and doesn't know.

CAYLEY: This is the first place in your work that you develop, at least at any length, the idea of concern.

What was the origin and the necessity of that idea for you?

FRYE: I think the word *concern* is roughly self-explanatory. I'm not using it in any peculiar sense. Man is a concerned being. I think that's one way of defining a conscious animal. As I went on, I tended to see a distinction between the primary concerns of man as an animal, that is, food and sex and property and freedom of movement, and secondary concerns, which are religious belief, political loyalties, and everything ideological. It seems to me that literature has a profound and, well, a primary connection with primary concerns. That is what distinguishes it from ideology and rhetoric of all kinds.

CAYLEY: How do you read the history of ideas in the light of these two concepts?

FRYE: The primary concerns, which I think literature deals with, are the concerns of man as an individual. You can learn a great deal about the ideological or religious structure of a society from a novelist like Flaubert or Zola or Tolstoy, but in the work of fiction they have to be subordinated to making love and making a living and getting on with your life — the questions of survival.

CAYLEY: In *The Critical Path* you describe a tension between what you call a myth of concern and a myth of freedom. What did you mean by these terms?

FRYE: As a matter of fact, I'm not entirely happy with the phrase "myth of" any more. I had a discussion with Max Black of Cornell when I was staying there for a couple of months, and I realized that that was not really a proper description of what I was talking about. I wouldn't, I think, use the phrase "myth of concern" now. I would speak more of concern expressing itself in myths.

CAYLEY: What I was getting at was the idea that, as Kant says, only the middle way is open. Freedom by itself becomes parasitical. Concern by itself leads to ideological domination.

FRYE: Every society is dominated by an ideology. When Marxism began, it professed to be something of an escape from ideology and said it would not set up a structure of authority. It would be something in which the state would wither away. But that didn't happen, because all ideologies are contained within a mythological framework. As long as people don't realize that, they will simply shift the emphasis without actually getting anywhere. Ideology is militant and builds up empires and class structures. It's an ideological concern that sends the Russian tanks into Czechoslovakia and the American troops into Viet Nam. If there's one thing clear about the late twentieth century, it is that it's an age where primary concerns have got to become primary or else. I mean that food and sex and freedom of movement and property, in the sense of what is proper to individuality, are the primary concerns. We must come to terms with those.

CAYLEY: Could we look at artists in different periods in relation to ideological concern?

FRYE: Artists have always been told that they have no real authority, that they live in a world of let's pretend, and that they just play around with fictions. Their function is to delight and instruct, as Horace says. They can learn from their own art how to delight, but they can't learn how to instruct unless they study philosophy or theology or politics. As a literary critic, I've been fighting that notion all my life.

CAYLEY: How have poets made space for themselves in the face of this view?

FRYE: Well, I think poets have to come to terms with the ideological structures of their time, particularly if they can't find any source of encouragement to believe in the validity of what they're doing in its own right. Again, from the eighteenth century on you get almost every decade something thrown up in the arts that is antiestablishment. But the goliardic poets and others in the Middle Ages also had to confront authority. The poets in the Middle Ages, for example, invented the code of love, which was something that ran parallel with the Christian religion and just got by ecclesiastical authority. The authority didn't like it, but it was there. The poets refused to budge. Dante starts with that. He winds up with divine grace in the presence of God, but he starts out with Beatrice.

CAYLEY: So the poets in this sense are a kind of loyal opposition — or at least as loyal as they have to be. What does Renaissance humanism represent by way of an accommodation to ideological concern? How does it manage it?

FRYE: The Renaissance humanist comes to terms with the Renaissance prince, much more obviously in Ben Jonson or Racine than in Shakespeare, who stuck very closely to his job as dramatist. Again, they go along with what the ideological authorities of their time say they have to go along with. But there is also in humanism itself a belief in the power of words. They called it style, the sense that it makes such an immense difference how you say something. This, again, sets up a claim of independence for the writer.

CAYLEY: So again you have a tension?

FRYE: Yes.

CAYLEY: Now when you reach the Romantic period, that ideological authority is overthrown?

FRYE: Not always overthrown. A great many Romantic poets still come to terms with the ideology, because there were conservative Romantics as well as radicals, like Blake and Shelley. But you're quite right. For the most part, the poet does claim that being a poet gives him an authority independent of ideological pressures. Goethe certainly thought that.

CAYLEY: What does that do to the role of the critic, then, in the post-Romantic period? How does the critic's role change when he no longer mediates between literature and the structure of authority?

FRYE: There is still the poet and his society, and there is still the poet responding to various ideological currents, even if he takes an independent view of them. So that the critic interested in the history of ideas has to deal with that in Goethe just as he has to deal with it in Dante.

CAYLEY: One of the people to whom you're sometimes compared, or said to be in the lineage of, is Matthew Arnold. Do you recognize the link?

FRYE: I have a strong affinity with Arnold when he says that culture is the ultimate authority in society and that all the class struggles between the barbarians, which is what he calls the aristocracy, the Philistines, which is what he calls the middle class, and the populace or the proletariat — all these are really subordinate to the authority of culture, even though culture may be impotent to impose its authority and, in fact, would be false to itself if it did. But, Arnold says, culture left to itself would move in the direction of a classless society.

CAYLEY: What does he mean by culture?

FRYE: He calls it the best that has been thought and said, but what he has in mind is an educational ideal. I would give much more prominence to the arts and less to the sort of nineteenth-century classical training than he does. But with all that, I'm quite solidly with Arnold. The trouble is that Arnold called himself a liberal, but he funked a great many of the liberal issues of his day. I feel he didn't really pull his weight as a liberal.

CAYLEY: Is that because this ideal, this idea of culture, still ultimately depends on there being gentlemen who can play the game? Is that what you mean?

FRYE: No, I just mean, for example, that Bishop Colenso attacked the historicity of the Book of Exodus, saying that if you think of the Israelites wandering around in the wilderness for forty years without their shoes even wearing out you begin to suspect that there are certain elements that prevent the Exodus from being a really reliable historical narrative. Now everybody knows that that's true, and Arnold knew that it was true, but somehow or other he thought it was a little ungentlemanly to say so right out in public where vulgar people might read the statement.

CAYLEY: So, like Mill, his confidence in the people is sometimes pretty shaky?

FRYE: Well, Mill was a much more genuine liberal.

CAYLEY: But still, Mill suffers from tremendous anxieties about what the consequences of his views coming to fruition might be. Mill and Arnold are akin in that respect, aren't they?

FRYE: Yes, but the anxieties with Mill come from his recognition of the power of the classes and their immense desire to fight the other classes. With Arnold, it's more a sense of nervousness mainly about the populace, mainly about the lower classes. Arnold never quite got over the fear inspired in him by the second Reform Bill, which threw about five million extra votes on the British elections. He was afraid that some of the traditional values would be going down the drain, and that forced him into panics, which don't sit very well on his record as a liberal.

CAYLEY: Arnold's idea of culture as authority is a response to the overthrow of the traditional authority of revelation, of the society's original myth of concern. And the overturning of that ideological structure as the exclusive authority then leads to a parliamentary image of culture where the competing claims freely interact.

FRYE: Except that you don't overturn it, you transcend it.

CAYLEY: What's the distinction?

FRYE: To overturn it means that you bring another class into the ascendancy. The title of the book that I'm writing now is *Words with Power*, which comes from the remark in the Gospels about Jesus that his word was with power. I would add to the word with power all of the other arts as well. They have no physical power. Mao Tse-tung says that power comes out of the barrel of a gun. Now if that is your conception of power, the human race is not going to survive the twenty-first century.

CAYLEY: Culture is an alternative conception of power?

FRYE: Yes. It's utterly weak physically, but it's the only surviving power there is.

CAYLEY: It seems to me you've also been interested in an alternative tradition to Arnold's, a tradition in which the artist is a worker, as in Blake and Morris, and education a meritocracy rather than a way of producing gentlemen?

FRYE: Arnold really had no choice. He was working in the nineteenth-century British class structure, and, like Newman, he felt that education was there to produce the gentleman. That conception of gentleman is obviously obsolete now, and for a person brought up in a North American democracy, like myself, it never was an alternative. I always thought of the structure of society as a structure of workers, and I was never frightened by words like *elite*, because in a properly constituted society everybody would belong to an elite of some kind. That is, everybody would have an expertise that wasn't completely replaceable. Blake and Morris certainly thought of the artist as worker, as producer.

CAYLEY: So that doesn't leave the arts outside of society as being the activity of gentlemen or depending on the patronage of gentlemen. Blake and Morris, in a way, are precursors of the contemporary view that you said you had from the beginning.

FRYE: That's right, yes. Both of them, of course, ran

into paradoxes. Morris could run his business only when he was patronized by fairly well-to-do people, and it was only well-to-do people who could buy Blake's engraved poems. But those are accidents of their time. They don't destroy the conception of the artist as worker.

CAYLEY: You've described yourself as a bourgeois liberal and even said that people who aren't bourgeois liberals are still "in the trees."

FRYE: Or would be if they could.

CAYLEY: I don't quite understand what you mean by that. This seems on the face of it a strange statement for a social democrat and a Methodist and a populist to make.

FRYE: Well, the bourgeois liberal to me is the nearest analogy I can think of to a man who is sufficiently left alone by the structure of authority in his society to develop his individuality. Because he's a liberal, he doesn't become an anarchist, that is, he doesn't grab all the money and corner all the property in sight. He's a person who can relate to other people. He doesn't either withdraw from society or become a mass man.

CAYLEY: So the emphasis is not the same as Marx gives to the term *bourgeois* when he uses it to signify the hegemony of a certain class?

FRYE: The bourgeois liberal is capable of seeing himself as having a certain position in society. He's also capable of seeing something of the limitations that that situation puts him into. You can't avoid being conditioned, but you can to some extent become aware of your conditioning.

CAYLEY: And your identification with bourgeois

liberalism is part of your reaching back, let's say, to Mill or Arnold — not endorsing what they are in their context, but seeing them as ancestors?

FRYE: Seeing them as ancestors and as a kind of human type that is produced when society is left sufficiently open. Actually, what I mean by bourgeois liberal — and of course I'm being deliberately provocative when I use the term — is steering a middle course between the totalitarian mass man on the one hand and a kind of anarchism of the ego on the other.

CAYLEY: Is there no antithesis between the bourgeois liberal and the left-wing Christian revolutionary? Your biographer John Ayre sees you, I think, as a mandarin and a rebel in one skin.[136] Is there anything to this?

FRYE: There could be. In certain types of society, including, I should think, most of classical China, the mandarin could not be a rebel. The principles of Confucianism wouldn't allow it. I think it is possible to be both, up to a point.

CAYLEY: And you've tried it?

FRYE: Up to a point I've tried it, yes.

VII
CANADIAN CULTURE

CAYLEY: Are you a Canadian critic whenever you're writing, and not just when you're writing about Canada?

FRYE: I think what one is is very largely a matter of environment. The question came up when I was on the editorial board of the *Literary History of Canada*, and we argued a bit about whether, as I put it in one article, every European immigrant who stopped off in Canada for a ham sandwich on his way to the States was a Canadian. I said I thought that Canada was an environment, that it was a place where certain things had happened, and that anybody who operated within that environment was a Canadian, whatever his passport said.

CAYLEY: So that Malcolm Lowry wrote a Canadian book when he wrote a book in Vancouver?

FRYE: What he did in Vancouver, he did within the Canadian environment. *Under the Volcano* has claims to be considered within the Canadian environment. Brian Moore is somebody in the same position.

CAYLEY: How do you think the Canadian environment has influenced what you have done as a critic?

FRYE: I think it makes you less anonymous. You tend to get lost in a country as big as the United States, and you have to be frantically aggressive to make much of a sense of your individuality. But in Canada there's a small enough community responding to you — I'm thinking roughly of the cultured, intellectual community — so that you do get known as a person, or at any rate identified as a person.

CAYLEY: That would account for a greater flamboyance in some of the American critics?

FRYE: I daresay, yes.

CAYLEY: In an essay about you Margaret Atwood suggests that the size, the blankness, and the forbidding quality of the Canadian environment has something to do with your liking for taxonomies and large conceptual schemes. Does that make any sense to you?

FRYE: Yes, but I think she also had a larger spectrum than that in mind — that Canadians have been obsessed with communication, which took itself out in building bridges and railways and canals in the nineteenth century and in developing very comprehensive theories of communication, like Innis's and McLuhan's in the twentieth century.[137] I suppose I belong to some extent in that category.

CAYLEY: Could you explain how you belong in that category? That is, where would be the link with Innis and McLuhan?

FRYE: Well, Innis started out with a Lawrentian theory of Canadian expansion, with the fact that coming to Canada from Europe is a totally different experience than coming to the United States and with the fact that you live in what is, for practical purposes, a kind of one-dimensional country. It's just a long line of river and Great Lakes and railways from one ocean to the other. The difficulties within communication, within the very act of communicating at all, and the fact that the settlements in Canada are isolated from each other in geographical ways — these things, I think, have brought about certain affinities among people who have talked about communication in Canada.

CAYLEY: So your schemata are bridges and telegraph lines? Is that how the analogy would run?

FRYE: It would be a rather shaky analogy, I imagine, but I have looked at literature always as a kind of overall pattern, just as Canada, when you see it on a map as one color, looks like an all-over pattern, even though it is actually a collection of isolated communities, or has been.

CAYLEY: So you're motivated by a kind of rage for order?

FRYE: It's a rage for order, all right, yes. Order without hierarchy, because hierarchy creates a limited order.

CAYLEY: Order without hierarchy — is that a principle that comes from your response to the Canadian environment?

FRYE: That's a principle of mine, order without hierarchy. There has to be order, because order liberates. I've always attacked, as we discussed earlier, the whole business of value judgments, because that creates hierarchies in literature: this comes first, and that comes second, and so forth. That doesn't liberate.

CAYLEY: How do you begin to make order if you don't have a sense of hierarchy?

FRYE: The conception of order is a conception of the integration of knowledge, and the conception of hierarchy is a conception of action and stimulus to action. I think you have to have some traces of hierarchical order in any democracy, as far as the life of action is concerned, but you don't need it in a cultural context. A scientist, say, sees order in what he's doing. He keeps referring that order to his repeatable experiments or to demonstrations of some kind. That is not a hierarchical use of order. I think the same thing is true of literature. You have pump-priming operations, like the Canada Council when it works, but they are not hierarchical ones: they don't say, "This is the primary value we are interested in."

CAYLEY: We talked earlier about journeys by train, and you mentioned then how impressed you were by the experience of being in the Gulf of St. Lawrence on board ship. Was that when you returned from Oxford in 1939?

FRYE: Yes, in the 1930s you had to go by ship. There weren't any transatlantic flights then. I suddenly realized when I was in the middle of the Gulf of St. Lawrence that I was surrounded by five Canadian provinces, all of them invisible. You don't get that kind of experience anywhere in the United States.

CAYLEY: What did that image say to you?

FRYE: Well, it said Jonah and the whale, more or less. It was also the beginning of the sense that Canadian economy developed from a big Lawrentian thrust from the east to the west. It took on political shape with John Macdonald, who thought in terms of east to west movement, starting in Great Britain and going across Canada and federating Canada as part of the British empire on its way to India.

CAYLEY: Were you by that time already aware of Innis or Creighton?[138]

FRYE: No, they came later.

CAYLEY: Innis was already the chairman of the Department of Political Economy at the University of Toronto in the thirties, wasn't he?

FRYE: Oh, yes, I was aware of him as a personality but not as an author. His important books hadn't come out at that time. I really didn't formulate this theory until I wrote the review of Ned Pratt's *Towards the Last Spike* in 1952 for the *University of Toronto Quarterly*.

CAYLEY: How does your later idea of a "garrison mentality" in early Canada relate to this experience of being surrounded?

FRYE: I was trying to explain in that phrase the psychological effects, first of all, of the Anglo-French War for the possession of the country, and then of the anxieties and moral compulsions of living in small towns that were totally isolated, as Canadian communities were. I knew something of cultural isolation from having been brought up in Moncton in the 1920s. The phrase "garrison mentality" has a certain historical context, and the phrase has got overexposed. Like other overexposed pictures and images, it has got a bit blurred and fuzzy, because Canadians are now the most highly urbanized people in the world. So the garrison mentality has been replaced by the condominium mentality. The garrison had priorities that subordinated culture, but still it was a genuine social unit. The condominium is neither cultural nor social. It is perhaps another, well, threat is too strong a word, but it's something one has to cope with.

CAYLEY: It seems a tremendous threat to me, as someone who has lived in Toronto and had family here for many generations. Toronto seems to me a city that's desperately trying to forsake its past, its character. Suddenly there's this anxiety about being "world class." And now the latest refrain is that Toronto is becoming more like New York. This is usually said with a kind of prurient concern which claims to fear what it actually hopes for.

FRYE: Part of the point is that technological developments tend to a greater and greater introversion. As long as Toronto was a city of homes, of individual houses, it was possible for genuine communities, like the churches and the labor halls, to function. But they tend to freeze up in a town of high-rise apartments. There's hardly a community left. The television set is so much more introverted than even the movie, and the movie in turn more introverted than the concert hall or the stage.

CAYLEY: But to return to my earlier question: did you see the anxiety of isolation as different in Canada than it was in the United States, where small towns were also isolated?

FRYE: It was more intense, and there was the sense of being surrounded on all sides by a frontier, instead of having the frontier over there on the West, which was the American experience.

CAYLEY: This relates to the image of Jonah in the whale. In Canada there was never an established, eastern-seaboard civilization which then moved.

FRYE: No, there wasn't. There was a southern Ontario community, cut off from the prairies by the hinterland of northern Ontario (I'm speaking now, of course, of years ago); and the Quebec community, which was different culturally; the Maritime community, cut off by the upthrust of Maine; Newfoundland, with its insular status, cut off by the inland sea; and the prairies, cut off from British Columbia by the mountains. The absence of a seaboard meant the absence of that turned-out political quality that the British had and the seaboard nations — the French, Spanish, Portuguese, and then later the Americans — also had. Central Canada gathered around the Great Lakes, to use Plato's expression about the Mediterranean Sea, "like frogs around the pool," and that gave us what little cohesion we had, with these immense distances probing out on all sides.

CAYLEY: You've also suggested, I think, that this produced an inner, as opposed to an outer, frontier in Canada.

FRYE: Oh, I think so. I think the sense of introversion in the Canadian psyche is very marked, and it's a matter of making internal journeys and finding there are images there. If you look at Canadian poetry, you'll find that not decreasing with the advance of technology and communications and so on, but increasing.

CAYLEY: Is that distinctly different from the American approach?

FRYE: There's a distinction of emphasis, I think. It's very difficult to generalize as a whole, but, if you think of somebody like Walt Whitman thinking of history as a big machine that's winding up and catapulting the Americans into the future, it's so different in its attitude from this rather cautious, piecemeal ad hoc solution of one crisis after another in Canada.

CAYLEY: You have identified in early nineteenth-century Canadian writing an argumentative tone, which served as a barrier to its becoming a more fully literary expression. How does that relate to the garrison mentality?

FRYE: It means that your normal form of linguistic communication is an argumentative one. That is, you have in every Canadian small town half a dozen churches representing a set of propositions, and you used to have a conservative-liberal dialectic politically, which led to a good deal of eloquence and rhetorical passion. That was the way that Canadians instinctively used words. They didn't use them imaginatively or metaphorically.

CAYLEY: But why was the society so highly politicized?

FRYE: There wasn't anything else. If you're in a culturally isolated small town and if you've got political parties, one representing British imperialism, the other continentalism, the only thing you can do is argue.

CAYLEY: So it's the sense of threat that creates the argumentative culture?

FRYE: It's the sense of opposition. You see, every proposition is a half-truth, is a half-proposition. It contains its opposite. That means that using words as propositions is a militant use of words. To use words metaphorically is to get out of that militant dialectic. But it takes a good deal of security to get to that stage.

CAYLEY: How does Canada compare in this respect with the United States, which shared at least a partly similar environment?

FRYE: I think the same phenomenon can be found in the United States. But you also get in New England and to some extent in the Maryland-Virginia area enough security of cultural tradition, which enabled them to develop writers much earlier than we could. Also, there wasn't the linguistic barrier that there was between Ontario and Quebec.

CAYLEY: And presumably the Revolution tended to have a settling effect. After that, the Americans could get on with it.

FRYE: Yes, the Revolution introduced a kind of deductive pattern into American life. It meant that you had an eighteenth-century inspired document — a constitution — and you didn't touch that document: you amended it and reinterpreted it. In many cases it came to mean the opposite of what it originally meant, but that's what always happens to legal documents.

CAYLEY: But it gave that society a stable framework, whereas in Canada we just argued endlessly . . .

FRYE: And argued on an inductive basis. That is, what kind of ad hoc compromise is going to save this country from falling apart?

CAYLEY: So in the U.S. between the Revolution and the Civil War there was a relatively stable period in which a literature could take shape, a cultural stability in which writers like Hawthorne and Melville and Emerson and others could flower.

FRYE: Yes, there was a cultural stability. Also, the constitution itself came out of a very stable cultural climate, namely the eighteenth-century Enlightenment, which Canada never had any trace of.

CAYLEY: In Canada, by way of contrast, it seems that by the time you get to something it's already over. This is what I take your idea of foreshortening in Canadian history to mean. By the time Canada is independent of Britain, it's already in such a completely internationalized environment that it never really is independent. It passes from colony to postmodern international state.

FRYE: Yes, you get books like Lower's *From Colony to Nation*. But actually you find that in culture, at any rate, Canada goes from the provincial to the regional, which is the more mature form of provincial culture, without going through the national phase at all. Or rather, to make this more intelligible, *culture* is a word with different contexts. One context is the lifestyle context: the British pub and the French bistro and the German ratskeller are different forms of a culture of drink. Canada doesn't have a very distinctive lifestyle culture. Its culture is pretty much identical to the northern American one. But that's just part of the homogenizing of the entire world. Then there is culture in the sense of the historical tradition, the shared heritage, where Canada does feel distinctive and threatened by American influences, and feels that it is the daughter of a mother country in Great Britain. Then there is a third area of culture, the creative life of a country, its literature and painting and music. Particularly in literature and painting and film, Canada has had quite a distinctive role to play.

CAYLEY: As Canada, or as regions?

FRYE: Not as Canada, but as a collection of regions within Canada that add up to something Canadian. There are no Canadian writers, but there are southern Ontario writers, British Columbia writers, Maritime writers, and Quebec writers. When you add them all together, you get a Canadian culture with a distinctive feeling of its own.

CAYLEY: How can a country like Canada have cultural independence when it lacks political and economic independence?

FRYE: I think that culture has a different sort of rhythm from political and economic development, which tends to centralize, and that the centralization process has gone so far in the great world powers that the conception of a nation is really obsolete now. I think it is possible to be independent culturally because the cultural tendencies are tendencies in the decentralizing direction. If you talk about American literature, for example, you have to add up Mississippi literature and New England literature, and middle-Western, California, and so on, and the theme of a cultural identity immediately transfers you to a postnational setting. A regional culture as I see it is a culture of which the writer has struck roots in his immediate environment. There's always something vegetable about the creative imagination. And you can't transplant James Reaney or Alice Munro to the middle of Brazil and expect them to produce the same kind of work — they'd become different cultural vegetables in that case. And, with the poets of the Charles G. D. Roberts generation, there was really very little of that sense of region. The "Confederation Ode" of Roberts was inspired by a map, not by a people.

CAYLEY: Roberts was consciously trying to be Canadian.

FRYE: Right, and you can't be a Canadian by an effort of will. The whole conception behind it is too amorphous. "O child of nations, giant-limbed" — that's Roberts harrumphing about the Confederation era. But that's not poetry, that's not culture, that's not anything except a manufactured sentiment.

CAYLEY: So when do you see this regional centering of culture really begin to acquire strength and authority?

FRYE: The difference between the provincial and the regional, as I see it, is that the provincial regards itself as importing its cultural standards from somewhere else, either England or France. Many of the most effective influences are American, but of course no Canadian ever thought of the United

States as a mother country and never thought of
Canada as effectively in a colonial relationship to it.
So you import your standards, and of course the
standards are out of date by the time they arrive. The
nineteenth-century English and French poets may
use quotations from Tennyson or Victor Hugo, but
the texture of their work belongs much further back,
with James Thompson or Béranger. Then eventually
writers become more aware of international currents sweeping across the world, and those currents
bring with them the feeling that cultural standards
cannot be met; they can only be established by the
writer himself. So you take on international qualities
in style, which are not homogenizing qualities, because they take root in soils in different areas. Margaret Atwood, Robertson Davies, and Alice Munro
are very solidly rooted in southern Ontario, but they
are not, like Stephen Leacock, provincial writers in
the sense of being branch-plant writers. They use
international techniques and devices, but they are
very different from writers who use them elsewhere.

CAYLEY: So this is a function both of maturation
within Canada and of changes in international communication?

FRYE: Yes. You follow an international idiom in
order to mature and establish your own standards
instead of accepting standards from elsewhere.

CAYLEY: And from what writers do you begin to
date this change?

FRYE: If you read a book like Knister's *White Narcissus*, you see a very conscientious, carefully written book that nevertheless seems to reflect standards
established elsewhere — not techniques, devices, or

idioms, but standards. So I would call it a very good provincial novel. With Sara Jeannette Duncan's *Imperialist*, you're beginning to move from something provincial into something regional, and by Morley Callaghan's time, where he's taking on an international influence through Gilson and Maritain, of course, you've moved into the regional period, which has escaped the provincial. And from then on, it's an open field.

CAYLEY: You yourself have played an important part in opening up this field, first as editor of *The Canadian Forum*. When did you take that on?

FRYE: I was managing editor in 1948 to 1950 or thereabouts. But when I was on a Guggenheim year, the editor of the *University of Toronto Quarterly* asked me to take over the job that E. K. Brown had been doing of reviewing Canadian poetry and making an annual survey of it. And from 1950 to 1960 I read all the poetry published in English Canada.[139]

CAYLEY: How did you see your role in those years?

FRYE: As a nurse, that is, as somebody bringing along a culture that was not yet wholly mature but showed so many signs of it. And that was why I said that I dealt with Canadian poetry for the reader of the *Quarterly* as though no other poetry were available to him.

CAYLEY: How was that received?

FRYE: Well, up and down. It depended on what I said, of course.

CAYLEY: It's possible to resent a nurse, someone who has seen your destiny but doesn't think you're achieving it.

FRYE: Yes, especially when you come along and

stick a needle in, as I had to do from time to time when people confused violent statements with the structures of myth and metaphor. Of course, a lot of people insisted that I was merely plugging a group of poets, whom they called the Frye or mythical school.

CAYLEY: Who would have been included in that group?

FRYE: In the fifties, Jamie Reaney, Jay Macpherson, and George Johnston particularly.

CAYLEY: Those were people who were friends and colleagues in some cases, and there must have been some influence.

FRYE: There was. But I did my level best to respond impartially to every kind of poetry that I was handed.

CAYLEY: How did your dislike of value judgments fit with your role as nurse?

FRYE: I'm working in a different area there. I think a reviewer has to make value judgments, knowing all the time that they're extremely tentative, but he can't get along without doing it because a lot of his activity is contraceptive. That is, he's trying to indicate to his readers what is likely to stay around and what has been really aborted at birth.

CAYLEY: So in that context you were inevitably functioning as judge and taste-maker, and you accepted that you were doing that?

FRYE: Yes, I accepted that I was doing it. It's only on paper that it's an inconsistency. In practice, it's not one.

CAYLEY: How do you see the proper relationship between critic and writer? You've rejected the idea that writers like Jay Macpherson or James Reaney were acolytes. But does the critic have some role in tutoring writers or in indicating to them a possible structure of imagery? What is the relationship?

FRYE: A critic knows that he's going to be read by poets, but he's not really addressing the poets. He's addressing the public, telling them what they will get if they read this poetry. The one thing the critic should never try to do is to tell the writer how to write, or to say that if he'd done so-and-so he might have written a better book. Occasionally you may suggest something like that, but that is not the critical function. The critical function is to take the book as presented and say what you see in the book.

CAYLEY: Do you have any concerns about Canadian culture today in the wake of the free-trade elections and the free-trade debate?

FRYE: I think there has been something of a golden age in English Canadian literature. French is different. But in the past, golden ages have had a tendency not to last. I know there's the constant tendency from publishers to keep on pushing for the Agatha Christie syndrome, that is, to produce commercial best sellers. Canadian authors have responded to that and have produced extremely good books that were at the same time commercial best sellers. But it is a terrific strain on the writer to ask him to carry off that kind of double first, so to speak. The people at the top, the well-known established writers, Atwood, Davies, Findley, Munro, and others, seem to be able to do it almost indefinitely, but whether you can ask for a continuous supply of such writers is another matter.

CAYLEY: It seems to me you might be saying that there's a risk to them too, that Margaret Atwood, for example, has to write another Margaret Atwood novel and that this inhibits her ability to experiment, to grow, to expand. Is this part of what you're saying?

FRYE: It may be part of what I'm saying, yes. I think that every writer who is established has to take risks, the risk of repeating himself, the risk of deviating from himself, and so forth. The thing is that the bigger you are the more you have to take risks.

CAYLEY: Your answer on the face of it doesn't seem to relate to free trade.

FRYE: Well, I think it's the natural tendency of political and economic movements to centralize. I know that there are books called *Small Is Beautiful*, but they don't apply to Canada. Insofar as books are a cottage industry, there's still a chance for Canadians to fight for their own cultural autonomy. To the extent that they're commercial products, there's a tendency to homogenize. We set up the Canadian Radio-Television and Telecommunications Commission (CRTC) in the Broadcasting Act of 1968 because we had sold the film industry, and the literary industry as well, pretty well down the American river. We've got some of it back. But I think that free trade does pose a certain threat to the cultural autonomy of Canada.

CAYLEY: You're saying that unless we maintain the tradition of a strong central state with the ability to protect and foster Canadian culture . . .

FRYE: Unless we believe in it, and the present government I don't see as believing.

CAYLEY: How do you see the role of the critic today, then, in the light of what we have been talking about?

FRYE: When I was doing the surveys of Canadian poetry in the fifties, I saw a maturing process going on that I thought would eventually produce more and better work. But now one has to think more of fighting a rear-guard action, which in fact the humanities have been fighting ever since the Old Stone Age.

CAYLEY: You've been teaching at Victoria College since the late 1930s. Was it by design that you never left, except for an odd year now and then? Did it just happen that way?

FRYE: It just happened that way. I had to go through a period when I was getting a great many offers to go elsewhere. I know there must have been people who thought I was just playing with these offers, pretending to consider them. But that wasn't true. Some of them involved very serious and even agonizing decisions. The thing that began to grow in my mind was the feeling, first of all, of the religion I was closest to — the United Church of Canada. Next was the political party I felt most in sympathy with — the CCF, later the NDP. Neither of those can be translated directly into American terms. And then later on, when I became a better known public figure, I began to realize that there would be some feeling of resentment in Canada if I left. I couldn't let that influence me beyond a certain point, but the feeling that there would be a certain betrayal in my leaving had, as its flip side, the feeling that I was making a contribution here and I had a function here that I would not have had somewhere else. I also went through a period, which impressed me a great deal when I was principal of Victoria, of seeing so many academics who had gone from Canada to the United States wanting desperately to come back.

CAYLEY: During what period were you principal?

FRYE: From 1959 to 1967.

CAYLEY: That was a long time.

FRYE: A hell of a long time.

CAYLEY: And was it onerous?

FRYE: Yes, though I had an extraordinarily conscientious and able president over me, Arthur Moore. Because of him it was a tolerable job, but it was not a congenial one.

CAYLEY: How did you become principal in the first place?

FRYE: I seemed to be the fall guy, that was all. As the academic head of the college, that made some sort of sense. I've always been a bit of a pushover for anything that can be sold to me as public service. That was why I stayed for nine bloody years on the CRTC.

CAYLEY: It doesn't seem to have cut into your writing. You kept up a phenomenal amount of writing during that whole period, with books appearing almost annually.

FRYE: No, it didn't cut into my writing.

CAYLEY: How did you do it?

FRYE: Well, I had to, because my writing isn't something I run. It runs me. I have to do what it says, and I had to give it priority. There was nothing else I could do. That meant, of course, that I skimped a good deal on my administrative duties, but there wasn't any way out of it.

CAYLEY: And didn't sleep much sometimes?

FRYE: That's what people said, certainly.

VIII
THE EDUCATIONAL CONTRACT

CAYLEY: What has teaching meant to you during all these years?

FRYE: Teaching to me is a way of trying out ideas. I used to say that I could never believe anything I said until I had said it to students and watched their reaction. I've always found that teaching and writing fed into each other. I made up my mind almost at once as a lecturer that I wouldn't write any notes for my lecture until after I'd given it.

CAYLEY: You say, I think in the introduction to *The Great Code*, that you are employing the tactics of the teacher in that book. I have the feeling that perhaps you had been doing that all along. What is the relationship between the teacher and the writer in you?

FRYE: The teacher, of course, helps to keep the writer in touch with the public. I suppose in a way I've been one of Derrida's logocentric people, that is, a talker who deprecates writing. I don't really deprecate writing — I think that principle is nonsense anyway — but I felt as I went on, and more and more as deconstructive, phenomenological, and other critical schools developed, that they were getting to a point where they could only talk to each other. In fact, back in the *Anatomy* days, I said that criticism had a mystery religion but no gospel. That was why I tended increasingly to address a general cultivated public rather than the primarily scholarly or academic audience.

CAYLEY: I'm interested in your view of yourself as logocentric in Derrida's sense, as someone for whom writing follows speaking. I first heard that put into a principle by Eric Havelock, who I think must have been a friend of yours, when he was here just at the end of his life for the literacy and orality conference at Emmanuel College.[140] He suggested that the problem of primary education for him was that writing was being pushed at people, that people were learning to write before they learned to speak, and so the proper relationship, in his view, was being inverted. In an essay in *The Well-Tempered Critic* you seem to be saying something similar. Is that your view?

FRYE: I think so. Havelock was one of a group of people, including Marshall McLuhan and his student Walter Ong, who seem to be close to what has always been one of my educational views, that in teaching youngsters to write you throw a dead language at them and ask them to decipher it. I think the obvious way to teach a person to write is to listen to the way he talks and to try to give some shape and direction to that talk as it goes on. There's a great current of verbal energy that comes out of any child, and the thing to do is to direct that, not to lead him into a sort of rat's maze of subjects and predicates and objects before his time.

CAYLEY: Well, we do see an extraordinary amount of dead prose in the world at the moment. I know there are more people writing than ever before. But do you think that might relate to your idea that this current of energy is not present in the writing?

FRYE: Yes. One thing I've attacked all my critical life is the notion that prose is language of ordinary speech. The language of ordinary speech is associative, and prose is a very highly skilled, sophisticated form of writing. Almost nobody speaks prose. It's a written form, but people who approach it without having trained their speaking style, I think, give the impression of deciphering something from Linear B. They write what is in effect for them a dead language.

CAYLEY: After I heard Havelock, I began to look back at the prose of, say, Dickens or De Quincey, and I found that in sentences that were a paragraph long and that were incredibly convoluted I could still hear a speaking voice inside them.

FRYE: Yes, it's not dead prose.

CAYLEY: And with you as well it's very evident that

a voice is speaking. What does metaphor have to do with the way you write?

FRYE: Everything.

CAYLEY: Can you explain how?

FRYE: I think I am a critic who thinks as poets think — in terms of metaphors. If you like, that's what makes me distinctive as a critic. I don't say that there aren't other critics who think metaphorically, but I do. And I think that whatever success I have as a critic I have because I can speak the language of metaphor with less of an accent than a good many other critics can.

CAYLEY: What does it mean to say that you think metaphorically? Could you contrast it with another way of thinking?

FRYE: Most modes of thinking in words are founded on the subject-object split, the thing that Blake called the cloven fiction. A descriptive writer, a scientist or a historian, works with a body of words and a body of events or things out there, and one reflects the other. A logical writer is writing so that one statement follows out of it predecessor. The rhetorical writer writes to produce a kinetic effect on his reader. But the poet is the person who enters into a world where subject and object have become the same thing. They're different aspects of the same thing. It's a very primitive language, but the poet speaks it.

CAYLEY: In reading your essays, I have the sense that they cohere but don't follow.

FRYE: If they cohere but don't follow, then the total structure would be something like a mosaic, where there is an overall pattern but everything fits, as

Milton would say, contiguously rather than continuously.

CAYLEY: And is that how you see them yourself? Is that what you think you're doing?

FRYE: There is a continuity, but that's in the chronology of my writing. I write one book after another.

CAYLEY: But if I take an individual essay, I see it as a whole permeating parts, rather than as an argument in which one thing leads to another.

FRYE: Yes, that's right.

CAYLEY: How does the aphoristic quality in your writing, which is very pronounced, relate to your method of composition?

FRYE: I keep notebooks in which I write very short paragraphs, and everything I write is the insertion of continuity into those aphorisms.

CAYLEY: Education and the university, it seems to me, are really at the heart of society in your view, and you've sometimes spoken about "the educational contract." I wonder if you could say a little bit about that and why you've called it the educational contract, with the implied contrast to the social contract.

FRYE: The social contract is not a historical fact, but it's a necessary fiction: people all got together in order to surrender their power to a ruler — that's Hobbes — or people all got together in order to delegate their power to somebody — that's Locke. In the educational contract there is a relationship of teacher and student in which it is the student who knows less than the teacher but paradoxically the teacher asks most of the questions. The process going on is the Socratic process, in which the relation of teacher to student as such is a somewhat embar-

rassing one, and you try to get over it as
possible in order to make a community of seats
That's how the contract takes shape.

CAYLEY: It's the teacher who asks the questions,
your view?

FRYE: Yes, for the most part, just as Socrates did.
The teacher has to pretend he doesn't know anything in order to communicate with or to educate his
students.

CAYLEY: And you still subscribe to that?

FRYE: Well, it's what happens in the classroom.

CAYLEY: But you do lecture?

FRYE: Yes.

CAYLEY: You've also said, perhaps trying to deprecate the vogue use of the word *dialogue*, that what
happens in Plato is that eventually Socrates gets the
bit in his teeth and everybody else shuts up.

FRYE: That's the next stage, because you pass from
the symposium stage to the lecturing stage. If I'm
lecturing on Milton, for example, the only presence
that has any business being in that room is Milton.
If I become an opaque presence myself and people
listen to me instead of listening to Milton through
me, then I'm becoming some sort of fake priest.

CAYLEY: Is the questioning stage the unsettling
stage? And then comes the lecturing stage?

FRYE: More or less.

CAYLEY: Is it possible to arrange things that way in
practice?

FRYE: You stumble into it. You have to stumble into
everything.

CAYLEY: People have spoken about the long pauses
in your lectures. What are you listening for?

E: I'm listening to the echo of Milton from my
dents. It takes a long time for that to penetrate, to
ercolate through to my students. People have talked
a good deal about these pauses, and the thing they
don't notice is that they come partly out of respect for
the students. I know that students are too serious to
ask questions just for the sake of asking questions.
When I teach, I try to transmute myself into a kind of
transparent medium so that the room in theory is full
of the presence of what I'm teaching, Milton or whatever. It's a long slow process for the students to realize
that they are in effect within the personality of Milton
and are not being talked to by me.

CAYLEY: How do you bring Milton alive in the classroom? What do you do?

FRYE: What you do, first of all, is expound Milton
and speak as though you were Milton until it becomes fairly obvious even to the dumbest student
that you're not. You expound him in a way that
obviously engages your entire personality. Somebody said that *Paradise Lost* was a monument to dead
ideas, and my comment on that was that there were
no dead ideas, there were only tired readers. I remember once a number of Catholic students from
St. Michael's came over to listen to my Milton lectures because for some reason or other nobody was
teaching Milton at St. Michael's then. One girl
stamped out of the classroom in a fury, saying she
was a Catholic and she wasn't going to have her
Church insulted in that way. I took that as something
of a compliment, because it meant she was confusing Milton with me. At the same time, I somewhat

respected the boy who turned to her and said, "Ah, shut up."

CAYLEY: And for you, what's at the very heart of education is coming into the presence of the writers you're teaching?

FRYE: Yes. The only authority in the classroom is the authority of the subject taught, not the teacher.

CAYLEY: Since you put it in terms of authority, can we talk about where the university fits into a free society as a source of authority?

FRYE: The university is the source of authority in society. It's the only one there is that I can see. But, of course, by authority I mean spiritual authority, the kind that doesn't give orders. The university and the church are the two different areas of spiritual authority. The university is where you go to learn about an authority that is not externally applied. It doesn't tell you to do this or that.

CAYLEY: You've often written about the unreality of the real world, and my sense of what you mean is that when one comes into the presence of Milton, to take your example, one then enters what is truly real. The educational journey is from unreality to reality in your view.

FRYE: Yes, the unreality being what's out there and reported in the papers, and the reality being what remains stable or improves. If I look over the seventy-seven years I've lived in this ghastly century, I don't see anything politically or economically that has not been part of a dissolving phantasmagoria. I see only one thing that has improved in that time, and that's science. I see only one thing that has remained stable during that time, and that's the arts. I would include religion with the arts, by the way.

CAYLEY: And can you say what you mean by stable?

FRYE: Something that's there and won't go away.

CAYLEY: So education leads people into the presence of this something that won't go away.

FRYE: Yes. Somebody wrote a book called *Shakespeare Our Contemporary*, and that means that Shakespeare is both our contemporary and his contemporaries' contemporary. If he is a purely seventeenth-century dramatist, you can study him only the way you do the stars, not getting anywhere closer to him. And if he's only our contemporary, then we kidnap him into our orbit and turn him into something that is not Shakespeare at all. He stretches over the whole period of time.

CAYLEY: How have you seen the university change in your many years of teaching? Does it seem the same world to you now as then?

FRYE: The university has reflected the changing social conditions. It's changed as society has changed. The nineteenth-century university was the very small college, which was the training ground for young gentlemen. That meant that all relations were personal: tutor and student had their private hours. As the university has come to reflect more advanced industrial and technological conditions — and of course the world is irremediably pluralistic in both the arts and the sciences — it has to be a world of specialists. It can't function otherwise. So you get a great deal of highly specialized scholarship, which makes a problem for the person who is still teaching undergraduates and who is still in that personal relationship with them. It throws more responsibility on the undergraduates too.

CAYLEY: You have always continued to teach undergraduates, which by itself is remarkable, given your reputation as a scholar. I don't know whether that's unusual at the University of Toronto.

FRYE: Toronto has always prided itself on its reputation as a university for teaching undergraduates. It hasn't always lived up to that reputation, although I think it's done better in the humanities than in the scientific or professional faculties. But the teaching of undergraduates seems to me to be where the action is. That's where minds are being opened and admitted to what I've always called the engine-room of society, where all the work is going on. I feel that the graduate school is the place where the good people ought to be teaching themselves anyway. It's also a very highly pluralistic, specialized, and, in these days, competitive school. So I find the undergraduate classroom really the educational center.

CAYLEY: What I'm wondering really is whether the university, as you would like it to be and as it must be to play the role you see for it in society, actually exists any longer. Is that university gone?

FRYE: Yes. The university as I would like it does not exist. The only thing you can do is fight rear-guard actions in small corners.

CAYLEY: Did it once exist? Or was it always an ideal?

FRYE: It was always an ideal, really. But where you have a small intimate college with students and teachers personally known to one another, you have the possibility of something close to the ideal.

CAYLEY: I see your idea of the university as having two dimensions, dimensions that are different but not necessarily antagonistic. You believe that education must liberate us from the unreality of the world. But I also see you as standing against many of the more conventional ways of understanding liberation. You're very strongly in favor of discipline and habit — sometimes you use the Latin word *habitus*. You've argued against the idea that education should be "relevant" or immediately gratifying. Some of this goes back to discussions that were going on in the sixties, and I wonder if you might talk about the ferment of the sixties, about the consequences of that time, and about the role you played.

FRYE: The student activism of the sixties was something I had really very little sympathy with. It started out with a group of students in Berkeley feeling that they were not being paid attention to as students, something I could profoundly sympathize with. As it went on they became more and more attracted by the clichés of revolutionary ideology. Then they turned into something which was no longer intellectual. In fact, that was the thing that sickened me about the student movement: it was an anti-intellectual movement in the one place in society where it had no business being. Once a student gets on a self-righteous kick, he becomes utterly impervious to argument because he's still too young and insecure to listen to anything except the applause of his own conscience. I knew that that movement would fall dead in a very short time because it had no social roots. It wasn't like feminism or black emancipation, movements with real social causes behind them.

CAYLEY: How was it anti-intellectual?

FRYE: It was anti-intellectual in that it used the anarchist and neofascist tactics of breaking up meetings and occupying buildings. They felt they were doing something when they were engaging in that kind of nonsense.

CAYLEY: The element of desperation in the student movement was something you could understand, I think — the feeling of unreality in the world that was provoking their reactions. You sympathized with that?

FRYE: Yes, but it was a counter-unreality that they were thrusting toward. What I find hopeful about the present political situation all across the world is the gradual loss of belief in the validity of ideology qua ideology.

CAYLEY: What was your advice to students at that time? What was the way you wanted students to take?

FRYE: It was the way of the intellect and the imagination. Those are the powers that you're given and the things you're responsible for.

CAYLEY: How did you respond to the demand for relevance? What did that slogan mean to you?

FRYE: I said that it was a favorite word of Nazis.

CAYLEY: Meaning?

FRYE: Meaning that the student radicals were going in a neofascist direction. The Nazis talked about *Fachwissenschaft*, about target knowledge, and sooner or later the useful came to mean what was essential for waging war. That attitude not only destroyed art and science in Germany for a whole generation; it also helped materially in losing the war for the Germans.

CAYLEY: You did, I think, sympathize with the spiritual crisis, the crisis of faith, that was behind the student movement. But you saw in the demand for relevance, if I understand you, a dangerous illusion.

FRYE: Yes, the demand for relevance was, to my mind, the absolute antithesis of what education is about. Education is a matter of developing the intellect and the imagination, which deal with reality, and reality is always irrelevant.

CAYLEY: This brings us back to *habitus* and the idea that you can't climb the ladder of imagination without practice. You're saying — you may have even used the image in one of the essays — that the door is open but you have to walk through it.

FRYE: Yes. The demand for relevance, which was, again, an anti-intellectual movement among students, meant of course that they wanted every lecture, every classroom meeting, every gathering of students to be an exciting existential experience. They wanted to shuck off the steady repetitive practice, which is the only thing that does contribute to the real advance of either the intellect or the imagination.

CAYLEY: At that time there were changes in the structure of the University of Toronto too, notably those coming from the Macpherson Commission.[141] How did you see those changes? Did you speak to the commission?

FRYE: I did speak to the commission. But of course there was a great hysteria gripping the university, and nobody would listen to me, so I gave up. But I felt that what it led to was something that Macpherson never envisaged, and that was the abolition of the honor course on the grounds that it was elitist, one of the most absurd words ever invented. I supported the honor course because I felt it dramatized the principle that whatever you're learning is the center of all knowledge, so that it doesn't matter so much what you learn as that you should keep on doing it.

CAYLEY: I read the commission's report. I never had a chance to speak with Macpherson about it, but the commission did seem to recommend the dismantling of the honor course.

FRYE: Yes, I suppose it did, but I think Macpherson himself was very much taken aback by the extent to which the dean of arts at that time took the bit in his teeth and revamped all the honor courses. I don't think Macpherson quite had that in mind. Like Gorbachev, he never knew it would come to that.

CAYLEY: How did you see the consequences of that? Did it work out as you expected?

FRYE: The consequences were that the faculty said to themselves, "Now we've put in all this cafeteria elective work because the students wanted it." And the students wanted nothing less. Consequently, they had to set up another committee to try to reverse the direction and get back to what the educational-jargon people call a core curriculum. I don't know to what extent that improved things, because the courses still had to be changed all around to accommodate the Macpherson recommendations.

CAYLEY: I remember a recent conversation with

Claude Bissell about the Macpherson Commission in which he said that he thought the pendulum had begun to swing back toward the old honors philosophy.[142]

FRYE: It's come back to some degree, but it's much easier to destroy than to rebuild. "The evil that men do lives after them, / The good is oft interred with their bones."

CAYLEY: How do you find your undergraduates today as opposed to twenty years ago or even forty years ago?

FRYE: Of course, they don't have as solid a high school background to fall back on. In my day undergraduates could get through a university course on the strength of what they learned in high school. I don't think that's any longer true. The good students today have a kind of earnestness, a sense of intensity.

CAYLEY: And that's good?

FRYE: Certainly, it's good.

CAYLEY: You've also made recommendations for elementary and secondary education. What were your activities in that regard?

FRYE: It was an extension of my feeling of addressing a public rather than a specialized scholarly audience. I said in the preface to the *Anatomy* that any subject that can't be explained to an intelligent nineteen-year-old is not a subject. The only change I made in that statement was to push the age-level of comprehension down until it finally got somewhere close to kindergarten.

CAYLEY: And what was your interest in the curriculum? What did you hope to see established?

FRYE: You remember the great panic after Sputnik.

The American public thought they'd been gypped by their educators.

CAYLEY: I was in grade eight in the United States at that time — one of those being panicked over.

FRYE: The publishers woke up to this fact. Harcourt Brace was running an extremely profitable series of readers from grade seven to twelve. They sent me the books and asked me to report on them as educational material. I said that the books taught no literature, that all they taught was American ideology, the American way of life. I said that their only educational effect would be to freeze the cold war on the American side. They agreed with this and asked me if I would put out a series. I said I couldn't possibly work that into my schedule, but I got people who understood what I was driving at, and they did get out a series. You can read about this in John Ayre's biography. It attracted a great many teachers, but in the meantime, of course, the panic over Sputnik had abated. The old educators had crawled out of the woodwork again and the old formulas were coming back in. Harcourt Brace is still making a great deal of money out of the books I ridiculed and condemned.

CAYLEY: When you spoke at the opening of the Northrop Frye Centre, you gave me an image that I liked very much. You talked about the lumber room at Hart House, and said that you'd like to become a kind of lumber room for later generations, or even present generations. What brought that to mind?

FRYE: I don't know where the image came from. It just floated into my head. I feel that the university's teaching staff is made up of functioning scholars.

I'm a scholar, I suppose, but I am also a type of scholar. I do not devote myself to training graduate students to be scholars in their turn. So I'm just there as a resource person for students to explore and get ideas from.

CAYLEY: But I think "the lumber room" extends to those outside the university too, who are rummaging around in your books in a somewhat similar way.

FRYE: Yes, I think it does. I hope it does.

IX
TECHNOLOGY AND SOCIETY

CAYLEY: In his two most recent books, *ABC* and *In the Vineyard of the Text*, Ivan Illich suggests that during the 1980s a profound and shocking change has taken place in Western civilization. He summarizes this as a change from the book as world image to the computer as world image. In his view the computer has replaced the book as the comprehensive metaphor for knowledge and what it means to know. Obviously the book plays a central role in civilization for you. Do you see anything like this yourself?

FRYE: I see a good deal of it, yes, and I sympathize with much of what Illich is saying. I've often said that the book is the most efficient technological instrument ever devised in learning. I think it's more efficient than a computer ever will be. It's a model of patience because it keeps saying the same thing no matter how often you consult it. It's a stable thing. It is a growing point of learning in a way that I don't quite see the computer being. There are many superstitions about the computer I don't share. I think it is being looked at on a kind of phony Cartesian basis, a view in which the mind is opposed by a body which is a mechanism. Nobody worries about the fact that the automobile runs faster than the human being because only the body, the mechanism, is involved there. But as soon as it becomes obvious that the computer can calculate and in many respects think faster than a human being, people get the jitters. They think that something peculiar to the human animal is being invaded by a rival kind of alien, science-fiction being. I don't think that that is true. The computer is a tool, an instrument. The difficulty is in thinking of man as conscious and of having a mechanism attached to that consciousness, whereas man is primarily a conscious will. The machine has no will to do anything. It depends on being plugged in or turned on. Only when it develops an autonomous will can it become a fully conscious being.

CAYLEY: Illich, I think, is close to McLuhan in seeing that our tools don't just do things, they also tell us something about who we are. The same idea is in Eric Havelock when he says that abstract or universal conceptions of justice occur to the Ancient Greek mind only as a consequence of the new technology of alphabetic literacy. What Illich is saying now, I think, is that the very idea of a stable self is a textual idea which tends to dissolve in the presence of cybernetic technologies, where a more evanescent idea of the self takes over.

FRYE: I think that the computer, again, is an instrument, a machine, a tool, and extension of a being. Now, there is a most pernicious tendency in the human mind to project onto machinery the qualities of external autonomy. Man invents the wheel, and in no time he's talking nonsense about a wheel of fate or a wheel of fortune or a wheel as a cosmological force which is alienating him from himself. He invents the book, and he starts talking about the book of life, in which all your sins are recorded. He invents the computer, and God knows what he's projecting out of that. But it's all superstition.

CAYLEY: Marhall McLuhan was a colleague of yours. How did you see his influence when it was at its height?

FRYE: I thought that McLuhan was being praised to the skies for the wrong reasons and then, after the vogue passed, being ignored for the wrong reasons. I think there's a great deal of permanent value in McLuhan's insights, and I had a great sympathy with what he was trying to do. Unfortunately, he had such rotten luck with his health that he was never able really to complete what he had to say. That's why he has come down as a kind of half-thinker who never worked out the other part of what he was really talking about. He talked about defence against media fallout, for example, an immensely fruitful idea, which, as a matter of fact, we've been discussing for the last few minutes. That I would like to have heard more about. But, as he told me himself, he suffered such pain with the brain tumor that it just knocked him out. Months at a time, even years at a time, he couldn't work.

CAYLEY: Speaking of defence against media fallout, you yourself were on the front lines during your years on the CRTC. How did that come about?

FRYE: When I was asked to come on the commission in 1968, I was told that it was largely because of Lester Pearson's influence. He thought it would be a good idea to have a tame intellectual on the board. The first chairman was Pierre Juneau, a person for whom I had an immense admiration and respect. Juneau said in effect that he didn't really care whether I attended the hearings, that what he wanted me to do was discuss theories of communication with the research department. Well, I did that and I worked reasonably hard at it. But the CRTC, like any other government agency, was swept up in an avalanche of routine. The research department was so caught up in this routine that it almost disappeared as a research department. There became a gradual lessening of what I could effectively do.

CAYLEY: The CRTC was created with great hopes.

FRYE: Yes. When the Broadcasting Act of 1968 came out, it made a lot of sense. But it wasn't only bureaucratic routine that the CRTC had to cope with — it was one of the busiest agencies in Ottawa in that regard — but also the steady development of technological things, like microwave, which increased the degree and effectiveness of satellite communication and the degree and effectiveness of American penetration. It also had to deal with local autonomy and with the community channel, which the CRTC was trying to foster.

CAYLEY: So you see those ten years as a sort of rear-guard action against technological change?

FRYE: Yes, increasingly a rear-guard action.

CAYLEY: Could the CRTC have done anything?

FRYE: Well, it did what it could.

CAYLEY: Could it have done more?

FRYE: I'm not really sure how much more it could have done.

CAYLEY: What if it had refused to licence the Global Network?

FRYE: It did that for as long as it could. But the pressure was pretty hard to resist. Of course the CRTC had to answer to Parliament, which was more manic-depressive in its attitude toward these things than the CRTC was.

CAYLEY: *The Modern Century* is the main place where you try to address what our times have been like. How do you see the progress of technology? And why, as you said earlier, do you associate it with introversion?

FRYE: It just seems obvious to me that in the technological developments that I've lived through in the twentieth century, each new stage brings with it an intensifying of the introverted. That's simply a hazard which has to be overcome, but it seems to be obvious. In the stage play you have an ensemble performance for an audience. The existence of the audience as a consensus, as a group, is very important. With the movie, you still have an audience, but it's an individualized audience sitting in the dark. Then with the television set, you don't move out of your living room. Similarly, the ocean liner is a place for romances and endless discussions and social movements of all kinds. On the jet plane, you just sit there and the guy beside you sits there, and that's it.

CAYLEY: This growing introversion is not a happy picture. What are its consequences?

FRYE: It's a hazard which has to be overcome. I think that nobody quite realized during the unrest of the sixties that a great deal of it had to do with the panic caused by television and the need to absorb it. As time goes on people do absorb it and bring it under control. Right now, there's a similar fear that computers will increase introversion to a practically solipsistic point, where people will simply be locked up in their own private jails. Again, that's a hazard. It's something I think eventually we'll learn to control.

CAYLEY: Could you expand a bit on why the sixties were a panic caused by television?

FRYE: It's a matter of saturation with images. If you're totally dependent on visual images, it causes a good deal of confusion. Is that stone dame over there Venus or Juno or Minerva? If it's a matter of hearing, you don't have that particular problem. But the saturation of images certainly dissipates one's sense of identity, until one begins to get control of it.

CAYLEY: And that control is beginning to be evident to you?

FRYE: In the course of time, yes. The machine becomes more and more what it ought to be, an extension of a personality and not an independent personality set over against you.

CAYLEY: You've described modern society as a skyscraper.

FRYE: As a Tower of Babel.

CAYLEY: Why do you think that's a relevant contemporary image?

FRYE: In the Book of Genesis we're told that the Assyrians or Babylonians or whatever people the author has in mind decided to build a tower to reach heaven. That meant that on a physical basis you were trying to get to a spiritual level, and the result of that was the confusion of language or conflicting tongues. I think every structure in human civilization has something of that quality about it: the difficulty of not understanding one another. You asked me about other schools of criticism, and the fact is that I don't so much disagree with them as simply fail to understand them. They're speaking their language; they have a right to. I'm speaking mine; I have a right to. But there's something in the construction of critical language that becomes more and more intensely specialized.

CAYLEY: If the different languages can be understood as images of introversion, and we understand each other less and less, how can commonality come back into our lives?

FRYE: As I say, it's a process which society, left to itself, can control. If you think how much time people spent staring at movies or listening to the radio in the twenties, and how much time they spend today watching television, you see that we've got a series of technological cycles. Each one seems to begin with something extremely primitive, but the technology matures. Eventually, you just get control of it.

CAYLEY: I myself have never been so pessimistic about this as in the last two years.

Frye: Pessimistic in what sense?

Cayley: About the inability to get control of it, about the increasing evidence that it gets control of us. I have a sense that we're moving toward a society of cybernetic organisms — "cyborgs."

Frye: That's a hazard. You notice in Orwell's *1984* the role of the telescreen. That's a technological development that a structure of power grabbed hold of, and that froze the technology at that point. The danger comes when the technology is frozen at a certain point. There isn't as much danger of its enslaving society when the way is left open for further developments, as I think it will be.

Cayley: In *The Modern Century* you also introduced the idea of an open mythology. What did you mean by this?

Frye: I suppose when I spoke of open and closed mythologies, I was thinking partly of Popper's open society, and also of what has later become in my thinking the distinction between the imaginative, poetic mythology and the ideological form of it.

Cayley: How does one live in an open mythology?

Frye: An open mythology is one where there is an atmosphere of criticism and where there is room for the imagination to have free play and all the other things we associate with cultural freedom.

Cayley: It means entertaining what might be true?

Frye: Yes, and as distinct from a closed mythology, where the authorities say, "This is it; this is what you must believe."

Cayley: An open mythology requires a kind of maturity.

FRYE: It's certainly more difficult, but then difficulties are a part of the responsibility that one takes on with freedom.

CAYLEY: Today society is continually dissolving and reforming. People's beliefs are at best provisional. The social order seems to be a phantasmagoria, composed of what William Irwin Thompson calls noetic ecologies — communities that appear and dissolve and reappear and dissolve again. All of this seems as if it could be construed as an open mythology? The postmodern person, it seems to me, is someone who no longer has any anxiety about myth or belief, but who participates in all these provisional, ever-changing structures, perhaps without very much commitment. I'll give you a very concrete example. Not long ago, shortly after I had been reading what you say about technology and introversion in *The Modern Century*, I happened to be on the street beside a young woman who had a most extraordinary appearance. I can't remember what it was: she had green hair or bobby pins through her cheeks or something. My first thought was that I wouldn't be able to appear in public like that. But then it occurred to me that she didn't necessarily think of herself as appearing in public in the sense of appearing among people to whom she was at least implicitly related. Perhaps by her appearance she was communing with distant role models and was involved in a private relationship with things I couldn't see. We might be standing beside each other on the street, but there was no relationship between us that could possibly embarrass her. Couldn't this also be an image of an open mythology with everyone, as Tocqueville says, "enclosed in the solitude of his own heart"?

FRYE: I think what you're pointing to is a tendency in the human mind to resist an open mythology, with all its difficulties and responsibilities, and to head for some kind of closed mythology. So the dissolving phantasmagoria that we mentioned as a feature of twentieth-century life is also a part of one society after another trying to close up — the Khmer Rouge in Cambodia or the Nazis in Germany, for example. And the fact that it can't last doesn't make it any better for the people who have to live under it in the meantime. In a society with more tolerance, a great percentage of that tolerance is going to be indifference, certainly. Freedom is going to mean for many people freedom to be apathetic, in other words, to live as though they're in a closed society. Then subsocieties get formed — the hippies or the punk rock people, who are actually living in societies which are as conventionally closed as they can get — and such groups have a greater sense of security by being closed.

CAYLEY: So an open mythology can terminate in either apathy or aspiration.

FRYE: Yes. We've gone through history thinking of peace as meaning that the war has stopped, and consequently, a lot of people, when you use a word like *peace*, say, "Well, the world of peace sounds awfully dull. There'd be nothing to do if there's nothing to fight about." What I go for is Blake's "I will not cease from mental fight till we have built Jerusalem." God says in the Book of Deuteronomy, "Behold I have set before you life and death; therefore, choose life." Well, nobody, with all respect to God, could possibly say that that was a logical "therefore." A lot of people who choose life choose it only because they have got into the habit of living. They find it easier to do that than to break clear of it. Others will choose life, but when life becomes an act of choice, then there's the question of what you're to do with it, what direction you're to go in.

CAYLEY: And you've chosen life.

FRYE: I suppose it comes down to the question that I cannot accept the pure arbitrariness of existence, or what Heidegger calls our thrownness. I think, to put it crudely, that there is a point in one's being alive. That would throw me back on my religious convictions, I suppose. I don't know how I can put it more clearly than that.

X
THE BIBLE

CAYLEY: Have you read the Bible continuously throughout your whole life?

FRYE: *Continuously* is a big word.

CAYLEY: On and off? I mean, you haven't left it alone for any long period of time.

FRYE: No, I don't think I have. For one thing I've always been teaching or writing about intensely biblical people.

CAYLEY: How do you read the Bible when it's so familiar already?

FRYE: That is a problem, actually. I find myself reading the Bible less and less. More and more I simply spot echoes of it when they turn up in other books.

CAYLEY: Or recalling it?

FRYE: Recalling it, yes. What I do now largely is check the original text, the original Greek and Hebrew words.

CAYLEY: *The Great Code* — was that a project that was a long time gestating?

FRYE: Oh, yes. It grew out of a course that I started teaching way back in the early forties, when I found that my students weren't responding to *Paradise Lost* with the knowledge of the Bible they had to have if they were going to figure out what the hell was going on in the poem. So I took this problem to John Robins, who was chairman of my department, and he suggested my giving a course on the English Bible as a literary document. But I very soon found out that I didn't need to confine it to students of literature. Students in the social and natural sciences were just as interested. I found, too, that I would get response from people with a range of backgrounds — from Greek Orthodox to Communists — so it was obviously filling a need somewhere. People kept urging me to write a sort of handbook to the Bible for students, but I kept putting it off because of my lack of scholarly background. I was not a biblical scholar. I was particularly weak in the nuances of the original languages. But eventually I realized I had to get it out of my system or bust.

CAYLEY: *Creation and Recreation*, written a couple of years before, already contained a lot of what you were going to write in *The Great Code*.

FRYE: Yes, I was moving in on it. If you're a knight about to kill a dragon, you better explore the territory first.

CAYLEY: Your subtitle for *The Great Code* is *The Bible and Literature*. And yet it seems in many ways to be about the Bible *as* literature. That is, you are discussing the Bible much more than you're discussing its later literary echoes. Why the subtitle? Is that a strategic disclaimer?

FRYE: I didn't want to write a book called *The Bible as Literature*. That had been the subject of so many footling courses, and there were also a number of books, good and bad, on the Bible as literature. They tended to take a sort of anthology approach to the Bible, to take bits and pieces out, like the Book of Job, that relate to other people's literary experience. What I wanted to do was deal with the entire narrative and imagery of the Bible and the impact that it has made as a totality on literature. That is why the word *and* was extremely important to me.

CAYLEY: So it's not a strategic disclaimer to fend off charges that you're poaching on theological territory?

FRYE: It was partly that as well. I wanted to make it clear that I was dealing with the Bible's relation to literature, that it was written mostly in literary language, and that it was neither an aesthetic literary approach to the Bible nor a doctrinal one.

CAYLEY: Your title comes from Blake, who speaks of the Bible as "the Great Code of Art." In other places in his work Blake goes even further. He says, for example, that Christianity is art, and there's another passage where he says that only a poet, a painter, or an architect can be a Christian.[143] What do these things mean?

FRYE: He meant that a man is not taking seriously

what the Christian religion is all about unless he's a creative and imaginative person. The word *artist* is a metaphor. You don't really have to be a painter or a poet or an architect to be a Christian, but you have to understand what an imaginative and creative approach to religion is.

CAYLEY: You have to recreate the Bible?

FRYE: Yes.

CAYLEY: You begin *The Great Code* with an idea adapted from Vico which you think sheds light on the language of the Bible. Vico envisions history as a spiral form in which an age of gods is followed by an age of heroes, an age of men, and then a *ricorso* or return. You apply this sequence to language, which yields the metaphoric, the metonymic, and the descriptive as its three phases. Beginning at the end, what is descriptive language?

FRYE: In ordinary speech, we use words to represent things outside the structure of words. But as a technique of writing, descriptive prose is a fairly late development because it depends on a technology. You can't write history until you have historiography and archives and documents. And you can't do science until you have a machinery for experimentation. You can't write descriptively in any sort of mature or fully developed way until you've established these things. Consequently, I wouldn't put descriptive language as a continuous form of prose much earlier than about the seventeenth century.

CAYLEY: What is happening before that?

FRYE: First of all, you get the logical language that developed out of Plato and, more particularly, Aristotle, where the criterion of truth is in the integrity of the verbal structure rather than in its relation to something outside. Aristotle was a very descriptive-minded writer, but he didn't have the technical equipment available to carry out his observations, say, on the generation of animals.

CAYLEY: Can you explain what you mean by saying that the integrity is within the linguistic structure?

FRYE: I'm speaking of the logical way of writing where sentence B must follow sentence A according to certain rules.

CAYLEY: So the syllogism is the archetype of this way of writing?

FRYE: The syllogism is at the center, yes. The criterion of truth is, again, not a descriptive one. The words are not being related to external facts so much as interrelated around the argument.

CAYLEY: So the question of whether these things exist outside of the writing doesn't arise?

FRYE: It arises, but it arises incidentally. The essential criterion of truth is whether you described it logically, not whether your description itself is accurate.

CAYLEY: Moving back one stage, what does one find before Platonic or Aristotelian dialectic came into existence?

FRYE: Socrates was a person who wanted to examine things dialectically. That is, you make a statement and you cut off the opposite of the statement if it's false. And you arrive at truth by argument with him in dialogue form. The people before Socrates were actually raising questions that move in the direction of science — questions about the four elements, about the nature of the stars and heavenly bodies, about the nature of substance, and so on. But they didn't, again, have the technology to get very far with them, so they stayed with cosmology.

CAYLEY: And how does mythic thinking differ from analytical thinking?

FRYE: Mythic thinking is the earliest of all, the most primitive form of thinking. Consequently, the illusion turns up in every generation that it's something that will be outgrown, but we always find that if you outgrow mythical thinking, you end up by rehabilitating it. Mythical thinking proceeds metaphorically in a world where everything is potentially identifiable with everything else. Gods, for example, are linguistically metaphors. That's how they start out. You have a sea god or a sun god or a war god, where a thing is being identified within a supposed personality.

CAYLEY: So metaphor is an energy that unites?

FRYE: Yes, metaphor is the way of thinking that holds the personal and the impersonal world together in the form A is B. The point about metaphor is that it opens up a current or channel of energy between the subject and the object. The most obvious unit of both myth and metaphor is the god, because the god is a ready-made metaphor. If you say Neptune *is* the sea, you've got some aspect of personality or consciousness identified with something in nature. The gods are not just human projections on nature, they're evocations of the powers of nature.

CAYLEY: Is metaphor the original form of human thought?

FRYE: I think it's where the use of words begins,

and I think it's where it's likely to end. What evidence there is indicates that human consciousness shaped itself out of animal consciousness, which of course is totally and completely identified with its natural environment, and the notion of a separate and subjective consciousness, which is watching and observing the natural world, is something that takes time to develop.

CAYLEY: Where does the Old Testament fit in terms of this development?

FRYE: The Old Testament is fairly late, and even if you adopted the most impossibly early date, even if you assumed that Moses wrote the first five books, that would still be late in the middle kingdom. I mean, the old kingdom of Egypt would be gone by then, and so the Bible sits on top of a very long historical development and it's already graduated from gods and nature spirits and these currents of energy in the natural world, and it is afraid of what it considers idolatry, that is, attaching something numinous, something divine, to nature and wants its readers to turn aside from that to human institutions and find their god there, and that means that their language has to be a language of transcendence, of something that turns away from the order of nature.

CAYLEY: So what does the Bible have to say to the contemporary revival of interest in the goddess, which you see in books like Merlin Stone's *When God Was a Woman* or Edward Whitmont's *The Return of the Goddess*?

FRYE: The reason for the Bible's distrust of all goddesses and female powers is that what they lead the mind to is the conception of the human being as an embryo wrapped up in Mother Nature and still unborn. The mother is the parent you have to break from in order to exist at all, and that is why the biblical god is male. Of course, one can take that and use it to rationalize patriarchal societies, but I don't think that's the real symbolic reason for the maleness of God in the Bible. So far as human beings are redeemable, man is woman. In Christian theology, the Virgin Mary has been given the place she has because she's the highest of the creatures, the things that are created, so that to the extent to which man can be reconciled with God, man is symbolically female.

CAYLEY: When you were studying theology, Rudolf Bultmann was talking about demythologizing the Bible. It would seem on your view of myth that this is quite impossible.

FRYE: It's impossible because the Bible is a tissue of metaphors from beginning to end. As I once told my students, there's a verse in John that says "Jesus wept," and that's about all that would be left of the Bible if you demythologized it consistently.

CAYLEY: You've said if you try to demythologize, you end up remythologizing. The result is always paradoxical. Can that be shown in modern Protestant mythology?

FRYE: I think it can be shown in Bultmann himself, because that's really what he does. He knows, as any competent biblical scholar must know, that everything, for example, said in the New Testament has its roots in the Old Testament. That means that while what is in the New Testament may be historically factual, it's not there because it's historically factual. It's there because it fits something in the Old Testament.

CAYLEY: So to reduce it to facts is meaningless, because the facts are all dependent facts organized metaphorically?

FRYE: Yes. You cannot approach the Bible beyond guesswork. You can't approach the Gospels, let's say, as historically factual narratives except by hunch. You get various films saying that Jesus was a married man or was in love with Mary Magdalene or went to Marseilles and founded the Merovingian dynasty. All of these are quite interesting as guesses, but they're not anything more than guesses, because the only source of the material is the Gospels, and the Gospels have no interest whatever in presenting Jesus as married or as in love with a woman or as having self-conflicts. They present him as a God on earth.

CAYLEY: What are the Gospels interested in, in that sense?

FRYE: They're interested in saying that the historical Jesus was in fact the Old Testament Messiah. And I use *was* because they were all written long after Jesus' death.

CAYLEY: This view of the Bible draws on a very old science of interpretation called typology, which you've helped to revive. Can you say what it is?

FRYE: The Christian Bible consists of an Old Testament and a New Testament, and the relation between them is, from the Christian point of view, that everything that happens in the Old Testament is a type of something that happens in the New Testament. So you get this tennis-game view of evidence. How do you know that the Old Testament is true? Because it's fulfilled in the New Testament. How do you know that the New Testament is true? Because it fulfills the prophecies of the Old Testament. After the Resurrection, we're told, the disciples confronted the risen Jesus and said, "We find this Resurrection very hard to understand." And he simply said, "Search the scriptures and you'll find that the Messiah has to rise from the dead."

CAYLEY: So everything goes in a circle? You can't find the beginning?

FRYE: Yes. That's the only evidence that the writers of the Gospels are interested in. They are not biographers. The one criterion they subject themselves to is that what happens to Jesus in their account must fit what the Old Testament said would happen to the Messiah.

CAYLEY: Now is this way of reading and understanding original with Christianity? Or is it already present as a way of understanding in the Old Testament?

FRYE: There is a typological structure within the Old Testament also. When Moses climbs the mountain and comes down again, he finds that Aaron has made a golden calf in his absence. Then later on you're told that Israel split in two, with the northern ten tribes and the southern two, and that the northern ten tribes set up golden calves or bulls to worship. One is the type of the other.

CAYLEY: Is this way of thinking distinctively biblical?

FRYE: It's distinctive with the Bible, I think. Typology is really a view of history. It says that history is going somewhere and that it means something.

CAYLEY: And the meaning always appears in the future?

FRYE: Yes.

CAYLEY: How is that different from other worldviews contemporary with the Old Testament?

FRYE: It's distinguished by having a temporal dimension that carries you beyond the surrounding environment. All ideologies are typological in the sense that they're all donkey's carrots. That is, they pull you forward to something that's to be fulfilled.

CAYLEY: Our normal way of thinking is cause and effect. The cause has to be antecedent to the effect. In typology, it's the other way around? The future is seen, in effect, as causing the past?

FRYE: Yes. In ordinary causality thinking, the phenomena around you are effects, and you immediately start looking for their causes, which are, of course, antecedent, so you're carried backwards in time when you're thinking causally.

CAYLEY: And do you see this anticausal thinking as unique to Judaism and Christianity?

FRYE: So far as I know, it's unique. At least it's the earliest form. There have been derivations from it since.

CAYLEY: How do you see its influence on Western civilization?

FRYE: I see it as introducing a temporal dimension into thought, which I don't think was there in anything like the same form in, for example, Greek culture. There's also a difference between the biblical and the Oriental religions. In Buddhism you have a compassionate Buddha and in Christianity you have a compassionate Jesus, but he's also a Jesus who confronts and condemns the world. It is a more militant conception of religion. It throws more on the will and less on enlightenment. That is, the crucifixion of Jesus is something that goes on every day. It goes on in El Salvador, it goes on in Viet Nam, and it goes on in Canada. The fact that the world is always trying to kill God is what, it seems to me, is distinctive of the biblical religions.

CAYLEY: Why do you call the biblical-Hebraic tradition revolutionary?

FRYE: I call it revolutionary because the Old Testament comes out of a people who were never any good at the game of empire. They were always on the underside, oppressed and placed in bondage by more powerful kingdoms, like Egypt and Assyria and Babylonia. So the central thing in the Old Testament is the liberation of an enslaved people, in other words, the Exodus. That liberation goes on repeating through the return from Babylon. In the New Testament it is again a struggle between Christ and the world, in which the world wins, to the extent that Christ is crucified and died and was buried. Of course, the central thing was the Resurrection. God can't die. Similarly, the Bible is monotheistic, but it's a totally different kind of monotheism from the kind you get in the empires — in Marcus Aurelius or the late Stoic philosophers. Those are imperial monotheisms.

CAYLEY: What does the eye/ear dialectic in the Bible have to do with its revolutionary cast?

FRYE: The metaphor of the ear — the voice of God,

God speaking — suggests an invisible God who nevertheless enters into you and becomes a part of you. The eye always retains a sense of the objective, the thing over there. In a polytheistic religion, like the Greek one, you have to have visual symbols, like statues, in order to distinguish one god from another. But if you don't have the problem of distinguishing among gods, if there's only one, then it's a reduction of that God to see him as an object.

CAYLEY: Does the word also become a command?

FRYE: It often takes the form of a command, yes. I think that the word of command in ordinary society is the word of authority, which relates to that whole area of ideology and rhetoric. That kind of word of command has to be absolutely minimal. It can't have any comment attached to it. Soldiers won't hang themselves on barbed wire in response to a subordinate clause. If there's any commentary necessary, it's the sergeant major's job to explain what it is, not the officer's. Now that is a metaphor, it's an analogy, of the kind of command that comes from the other side of the imagination, what has been called the kerygmatic, the proclamation from God. That is not so much a command as a statement of what your own potentiality is and of the direction in which you have to go to attain it. But it's a command that leaves your will free, whether you follow it or not.

CAYLEY: You have suggested that some of our difficulties with understanding God are language difficulties. Can you explain that?

FRYE: It has always been assumed that the proper language for comprehending the conception of God is dialectical or theological language. I think that's a valid way of approaching God, but its limitations and its context ought to be kept in mind as well. The motive for persecution is never "You must believe in God." It's always "You must believe in what I mean by God." And, of course, whatever the human being thinks of God is totally inadequate.

CAYLEY: But why, as you say in *The Great Code*, does Nietzsche's famous statement that God is dead refer to an event within the history of language?

FRYE: Nietzsche himself, after his lunatic prophet Zarathustra said that, scratched his head and said, "Well, it's going to be very difficult to get rid of God as long as we keep on believing in grammar." Believing in grammar, I think, meant for him primarily believing in subjects and predicates and objects. As long as the human being is a subject and God is an object, there will always be an unresolved problem in language. The metaphorical approach, on the other hand, moves in the direction of the identity of God and man. My interest in the Bible has led me to a growing interest in the way that nouns or the world of things rather block movement. The scientist, for example, is trying to describe processes in space-time, and ordinary language has to twist that into events in time and things in space. But these processes are not going on in space and time. One of the most seminal books I have read is Buber's *I and Thou*. Buber says we are all born into a world of "its," and if we meet other human beings we turn them into "its." In this view, everything is a solid block, a thing. Consequently, when we think of God, we think of a grammatical noun. But you have to get used to the notion that there is no such thing as God, because God is not a thing. He is a process fulfilling itself. That's how he defines himself: "I will be what I will be." Similarly, I am more and more drawn to thinking in terms of a great swirling of processes and powers rather than a world of blocks and things. A text, for example, is a conflict of powers. That's why the Derrida people can pursue a logic of supplement. They can extract one force and set it against another. But the text is not a thing any more. A picture is not a thing. It's a focus of forces.

XI
FAITH

CAYLEY: What's your relationship to the United Church?

FRYE: I used to describe myself as a United Church plainclothesman, meaning that I was in effect somebody who was attached to a church. Most undergraduates are instinctively agnostic and rather rebellious about churches and about religious institutions generally. I have always used a very secular attitude in order to win the confidence of people, not because I want to catch them in a trap later but precisely because I want them to understand that there isn't any trap.

CAYLEY: So you have not really ever been a minister except for those few months in Saskatchewan?

FRYE: Not really. The Puritans distinguished be-

tween a congregation and a church, and I feel that I
am a fully active member of the congregation, although my field of activity has been the university
and my writing.

CAYLEY: What is faith?

FRYE: Faith, according to the New Testament, is the
hypostasis of hope and the *elenchos*, the proof or
evidence, of the unseen.[144] I would translate that
approximately as meaning that faith is the reality of
hope and the reality of illusion.

CAYLEY: The reality of illusion? You put it rather
paradoxically. Illusion is something that is not real
by definition for us. Are you saying that faith means
believing in fairy tales?

FRYE: No, that's what other people say. For most
people, it's the schoolboy's definition. Faith is
believin' what you know ain't so. I have no use for
that kind of faith, and I don't think the New Testament does either. Faith is achieved through experience. The Wright brothers start to wonder if a
heavier-than-air machine can actually get off the
ground. Everybody says, "That's impossible, that's
an illusion." They get the thing off the ground.
That's faith.

CAYLEY: So faith is something that one does, something that one achieves, not something that one
believes?

FRYE: It's not an objective body of propositions.
The author of Hebrews, after he's given his defini-
tion of faith, goes on and gives examples from the
Old Testament. He says that by faith these people
did certain things. They weren't talking about a
Trinity of three persons in one substance. They

weren't saying that anybody who doesn't believe in the identity of the substance or the difference of the persons is *et cetera, et cetera*.

CAYLEY: When we talked about Blake a few years ago, you quoted Vico's Latin adage *verum factum*, that we can't believe what we haven't made.

FRYE: "What is real is what we've made."

CAYLEY: Now how does that enter into this understanding of faith? Is faith a structure that we make, in effect?

FRYE: It's a structure that we have made and can, therefore, remake. When you wake up in the morning, you dismiss the dream world of illusion for the reality that your conscious waking mind sees around you. But actually, that reality is entirely manmade. Everything in the bedroom around you is human in its construction, and whatever men have made they can remake.

CAYLEY: What does practice have to do with the achieving of faith?

FRYE: Practice has everything to do with the achieving of faith, because of the fact that all skilled effort, all constructive, creative effort, depends on practice.

CAYLEY: But in the area of faith, how does that work? It seems to me that your view implies that one would need, first of all, to strengthen the imagination.

FRYE: Again, faith relates to realization, and realization means, to put it rather coarsely, craftsmanship. That is, it's a matter of recreating your experience. That is something you have to acquire a skill in doing. The Gospel says that faith can remove mountains. It's no good just saying, "I have faith that

that mountain shall not be there." The next minute, of course, it stays there. So obviously you have to keep on working at your conception of faith until it becomes more precise and heads in the direction of realization.

CAYLEY: And moving the mountain doesn't necessarily exclude shovels. Is that what you're saying?

FRYE: It takes on shovels in the process.

CAYLEY: You have spoken of literature as a laboratory of possibilities and of myth as what might or could be true. I've sometimes had trouble understanding what that means. Does it mean what we could make true, in the same sense that you spoke earlier of illusion as something that we can make real?

FRYE: Yes. The criterion in literature is not the real. It's the conceivable. The conceivable means that there are many things that are not here but could be here. So literature is constantly a challenge to the sense of possibility, the potential.

CAYLEY: But what is the guarantee that what we make is not simply what we would like to be true?

FRYE: There's every possibility that what we make is what we'd like to be true.

CAYLEY: Is there any way we can know that we're not simply committing ourselves to our wishes?

FRYE: But you do commit yourself to your wishes. Most of your wishes turn out to be phony, but you just have to keep on going.

CAYLEY: In a critique of *The Great Code* in the *Toronto Journal of Theology*, William Fennell is troubled by your seeming to deny what he at one point calls "the objectivity of God."[145] He seems to be trying to get

around him, and he gets three of the most beautiful women who were ever seen for his daughters.

There's a touch of fantasy in that, which reminds us that tragedy is always something inevitable, whereas comedy always contains a concealed gimmick that you don't quite believe in. It takes an act of faith to believe in a comedy. It takes an act of faith to believe in the whole of the Book of Job, including the restoration at the end. It's even possible that if you'd seen Job, you might not have seen the beautiful daughters. You might have seen a beggar on a dunghill. But he has seen something that we have not seen and known something that we don't know.

CAYLEY: Why does God make the wager in the first place?

FRYE: Because he cares about human beings.

CAYLEY: How does the wager show his care?

FRYE: The fact that he's willing to risk his own credit as God by betting on Job's loyalty.

CAYLEY: So he's not toying with Job? He's not abusing Job?

FRYE: He's not playing with Job. Satan is.

CAYLEY: He's actually trying to deliver Job from his illusion, the illusion in which his goodness has landed him?

FRYE: He's trying to split off what is genuine about the human being, Job, from the world of Satan in which Job lives.

CAYLEY: And why is Satan allowed there in the court to begin with?

FRYE: We don't know, except that Job obviously goes through an evolution, which would have been impossible if it had not been for the disasters that Satan inflicts on him.

CAYLEY: Can you say how the events of Job illustrate what you said earlier about the vertical axis in our experience?

FRYE: As I say, God is presenting his creation to Job as an order, a cosmos, rather than a chaos. It has a top and bottom. It's different from the horizontal experience of time because it transcends that.

CAYLEY: It seems to me this is the prototypical moment in the Bible and in literature for you — the point where the horizontal path ends and one looks up and down.

FRYE: The horizontal path doesn't actually end. It keeps on going. Time has no beginning or end. That's the trouble with time. But the present vision is the one that extracts you from the tyranny of time.

CAYLEY: Does anything happen to God in the course of the book?

FRYE: Nothing happens to him except that he manifests himself to man.

CAYLEY: And that's the meaning of Jehovah passing into Jesus in Blake's illustrations of the book?

FRYE: Yes.

CAYLEY: Perhaps you could say how Blake's drawings illustrate this reading.

FRYE: Blake looks at Job as a kind of spiritualized version of the story of the fall in Genesis. That is, you start with Job doing his moral duty and, therefore, not being quite on the upper limit of what human beings can achieve. So he falls into Satan's world. Satan is young and vigorous, God is old and imbecile, and Satan takes over and dominates the world until Job goes through the vision of the morning stars singing together in Plate 14 and the vision of the Leviathan or Behemoth in Plate 15. The new creation and consequently the renewed God, who is among other things the divinity in Job himself, take over.

CAYLEY: You've called the Book of Job an epitome of the Bible. What does that mean? How does it epitomize the whole Bible?

FRYE: It seems to me that Job begins with a spiritualized form of Genesis. It ends with a spiritual form of apocalypse or revelation. And in the middle comes this vertical contact between God and man. The New Testament has a different version of this. It sees that contact as existing in Jesus. But imaginatively and mythically it's in the Book of Job.

CAYLEY: Do the two readings of the Book of Job that you've given relate to the conceptions of God as a noun and as a verb?

FRYE: The reading I disagree with, which makes God a bully who forces Job into agreeing with the justice of his ways, is the objective God who is sitting up there in the sky and is linguistically a noun. That is, he's an object that never changes. All he does is to say, "Look what I did in the remote past: I created this wonderful world." As I see it, the opening of the story with Satan in God's court depicts God shifting the center of action to Satan, who brings about all these disasters. Job then is driven to assert the dignity of human beings, at least in his own context. "If I've done so and so, then it's all right. But I haven't; therefore, there's a problem." At that point God moves in, and the new creation he displays to Job is the old creation again, but it's something in which Job now participates. It's something that engages Job as an actor, as an experiencer. That means that God himself has become a principle of action and experience. He has transformed himself from a noun in Job's mind into a verb in Job's spiritual body.

CAYLEY: Can we turn now for a minute to Genesis? One of the things that's going on in the world today is a search for a new nature philosophy. For example, within environmentalism a movement has emerged called deep ecology, which takes what it calls a biocentric as opposed to an anthropocentric view of things.[146] It seems to me that your reading of the Bible offers an interesting caution to this movement, and I'd like to talk about the Book of Genesis in that light. Can we begin with the Bible's account of creation?

FRYE: There are two accounts of creation in the Bible. The first one, the one with the six days and the day of rest, is a creation that throws the emphasis on structure and system. God rests on the seventh day, and thereby the creation becomes objective to him and therefore to man. This is an order that the conscious mind can study. I don't think that the first chapter of Genesis was ever intended to tell us how the order of nature came into being. I think it tells us how the cosmos dawns on a conscious human mind. Everything in that first creation deals with differentiation. The land is split off from the sea, the waters from the firmament, the light from the darkness, and man emerges at the top of the natural creation. Then you get the other account in chapter two, which begins with a garden and deals with animals as domestic pets. The imagery is oasis imagery. It's all gardens and rivers. And the emphasis is heavily on the distinctness of the human order. First you get Adam, then you get Eve as the climax of that account of creation. Obviously, that describes a state of being in which man and his environment are in complete harmony. Then comes the fall, which is first of all self-consciousness about sex, or what D. H. Lawrence calls "sex in the head." That really pollutes the whole conception of sexuality and thereby pollutes in the same way the relation of the human mind to its natural environment.

CAYLEY: Why is self-consciousness about sex the fall? And why is it particularly threatening to God? It's said, I think, that God is particularly worried that Adam and Eve have eaten this fruit and that they have gained this knowledge.

FRYE: When Genesis says that Adam and Eve have eaten of the fruit of knowledge, it means that they are now in a moral order founded on sexual repression. The great danger is that they may reach their hands to the Tree of Life. The explanation of Milton is one that makes sense at that point. God throws Adam and Eve out of the garden because if they eat of the Tree of Life now, they will live forever in a fallen world.

CAYLEY: Isn't there also an intimation of threat to God, and perhaps to other gods whom he seems to be addressing, after they eat of this tree?

FRYE: It sounds as though there was, yes.

CAYLEY: And why is that?

FRYE: I think that the grammatical structure of the sentence, where there is a kind of break, does indicate something very like panic in the mind of the Elohim. If man lives forever in a fallen world, then he is, in Milton's terms, demonic rather than human. The demonic is something that sets up a rivalry with God, instead of simply being disobedient to him.

CAYLEY: The fallenness of the world is something that is not actually in Genesis. At least, the idea that nature falls with man is not explicitly stated.

FRYE: It's not explicitly stated, no. But Adam is told to go and till the ground from whence he was taken. He has to struggle for his living in an alienated nature.

CAYLEY: So implicitly it's not a garden any more.

FRYE: It's not a garden obviously. In fact, the ground is cursed after the fall and remains so until the flood.

CAYLEY: Is this idea of fallenness necessary to your understanding of things? Do you accept it?

FRYE: It's necessary to my understanding in the sense that I think that there is great deal in human nature that is maladjusted to physical nature. I simply cannot believe in noble savages and that a harmony between man and nature is possible in the present state of human consciousness. But we are in the twentieth century gradually beginning to realize that exploiting nature is just as evil as exploiting another man.

CAYLEY: What I see in current thinking is an effort to construct a democratic philosophy that extends to the natural world, to see human beings as having no privileged place in this order, and to see nature in a pantheistic way, as a teacher, as our primary teacher. I think the Bible presents a stumbling block to this philosophy, partly because of the idea of creation. In the age of ecology, an immanentalist, Buddhist type of philosophy is more attractive, because it doesn't objectify creation and separate us from it to the same extent. Is this something that you've been thinking about at all?

FRYE: Yes. I think that the way the Bible deals with this question is confusing to most readers, because we've got two bodies of imagery to deal with. One is humanity versus physical environment. The other is the sexual image of man and woman. The fall was, as I say, a pollution of sex. Adam and Eve knew that they were naked and started to make clothes. Therefore, rehabilitation — going the opposite way from the fall — would be, among other things, a rehabilitation of sex. So that the relation of man and nature would become part of the relation of love, God says to man in the first chapter, "Now you're the boss of creation, you're the head privileged person here." The implication is that if you're the boss, you ought to love what is subordinated to you. Otherwise your authority is worth nothing. After the fall, God says, "From now on man is going to boss woman." It's explicitly said that the patriarchal society is a result of sin, a result of the fall. So that to go the other way would be to restore the original love relationship between humanity and physical nature.

CAYLEY: As between man and woman?

FRYE: Yes, but that precedes it, you see. In the Song of Songs the bride's body is a garden enclosed, a fountain sealed, that is, the inner paradise that has not yet become integrated into human experience.

CAYLEY: What your view has to say to the current

discussion, it seems to me, is that it's important to distinguish the two levels of nature: nature as sub-human mechanism and nature as it appears to illuminated vision. This distinction does not permit us simply to deify nature as such.

FRYE: The Bible regards the deifying of nature, of course, as one of the most dangerous things you can do. There's nothing numinous or worshipful in nature. It's a creation.

CAYLEY: So how do you view current attempts to rediscover the sacred in nature?

FRYE: I would share the Bible's concern. I don't think it's possible to locate the sacred in nature, though you may use images from nature in expressing sacredness.

XIII
PRIMARY CONCERN AND IMAGINATIVE VISION

CAYLEY: In *The Critical Path*, published in 1970, you distinguished between freedom and concern. In more recent writings you have distinguished between primary and secondary concern. What do you mean by primary concern?

FRYE: Primary concern is what man has as an animal in nature. He wants to eat, he wants to copulate, he wants to have certain things that are part of his individuality, such as property, and he wants freedom of movement. In the cold war you had, in the Soviet Union in the name of a supposedly materialistic ideology, food shortages, prudery, the abolition of all property, and rigid restrictions on freedom of movement. In the United States during the same period you had far too much food and drink and far too much sex and far too much property and far too much nomadism or wandering around. In other words, all these primary concerns were fulfilled without any respect for the fact that there's a mind as well as a body and that there is a sublimation process as well, a satisfaction process.

CAYLEY: Why have you argued that primary concern must now become primary?

FRYE: What I've said is the twentieth century is the century in which primary concerns must be recognized as primary, or else. In other words, in the past the desire to survive had to give place to the desire to go to war, to grab somebody else's territory. But you can't afford that kind of thing any more. It's not only that nobody could win wars. It's also that wars affect the actual survival of the human species on the planet.

CAYLEY: Could you paint a picture for me of a world in which primary concern has become primary?

FRYE: It never has.

CAYLEY: I know, but if it did? I'm trying to get at the difference between that kind of world and a world of hedonism.

FRYE: It would be a world in which the purely physical satisfaction of the primary concerns combines with the denial of these concerns in the interest of something which is conscious and mental and, if you like, spiritual. That is, a primary need is sex, but love is something of which sex is only a very small part. But the really primary concern takes in both dimensions.

CAYLEY: Primary concern has to be met because if

it's repressed, then everything else appears warped in consequence.

FRYE: I suppose I am saying that, yes. Everything which is excluded from the mind or from society will fight its way back in sooner or later. The thing is that it sets up a very destructive situation when it does that.

CAYLEY: What I'm trying to get at here is the opposition between discipline and desire. You've said again and again that people can acquire the understructure of freedom only by patient habit. And yet you emphasize the primacy of physical and emotional satisfaction.

FRYE: But there's no antithesis there, you see. Satisfying primary concerns on a purely physical level means depending on externalities for their satisfaction. It means that there is nothing at the center which assimilates. You're just a baby being fed. As you mature you become more and more an integrating force that assimilates things which make for survival, for love, for freedom of movement, and so forth.

CAYLEY: You assimilate them?

FRYE: Well, yes. If you're referring to me, I would rather be alive than dead, would rather be free than a slave, and would rather love people than hate them. That means that I try as far as possible not to be dependent on purely external things, because they give out sooner or later. For a conscious being concern extends over the mind as well as the body. I would rather be alive than dead. But what have I got to live for? When I start to answer that question, I'm in a mental world, in a world of sublimation. I want freedom rather than bondage. But what do I want freedom for? So that I can do what I must do.

CAYLEY: But how is the "must" given to you? Where does the "must" come from?

FRYE: The "must" is what you enter into from your actual situation. Jesus has a parable about the talents. The word *talent* meant a certain sum of money in those days. Now it means something that is a quality, something that's born in you. As we've known ever since Aristotle, in fact, thousands of years before that, everybody tries to fulfill himself, to fulfill his possibilities as a being.

CAYLEY: Primary concern expands as it is fulfilled. You don't see any necessary opposition between physical and spiritual satisfactions?

FRYE: I've spent most of my writing career avoiding either/or questions. At first, when I taught a course on the Bible, students in class would say, "Do you believe this or not? Answer yes or no." And I would say, "You know what you can do with all either/or questions in that framework." I just don't accept them.

CAYLEY: This comes back to why you don't argue. An argument has a dialectical either/or structure.

FRYE: The dialectical structure runs along an either/or framework: either this or that. So you exclude that, but the that is lying in wait for you, and pretty soon it has taken over.

CAYLEY: What's the alternative?

FRYE: You're in a both/and world, where, again, the "either" and the "or" have fused.

CAYLEY: But down here on earth we do often face

brutally simple choices in which "either" and "or" remain quite distinct.

FRYE: Yes.

CAYLEY: You can be a conservative radical in the world of ideas, but there must be a point in the actual world where you have to be one or the other.

FRYE: Yes, you're quite right. But you see, there's the area of knowledge and there's the area of experience. In the world of knowledge there is nothing new under the sun, and in the world of experience there is a time for all things. In the world of knowledge, I think there are things that get established, but the only either/or dialectic I am interested in is the apocalyptic one, which moves toward the separation of a world of life from a world of death. Not a separation of the good from the evil — I don't believe in that. When you make choices, when you make decisions, you are always moving toward an apocalyptic vision of something that doesn't die, and throwing off the body of death that you ought to be delivered from. I know it sounds as though I am dodging your question, but that's really very central to what I believe.

CAYLEY: Could you say a bit more about how an apocalyptic separation of life from death differs from a moral distinction between good and evil?

FRYE: In ordinary life the good/evil distinctions are hopelessly tangled. Jesus has another parable on the wheat and the tares, in which he says there's no use in trying to root out the weeds from the grain in this world. They're too inextricably entangled. So that the final separation of life and death has to be in the form of an imaginative vision.

CAYLEY: Has to be in the form of an imaginative vision?

FRYE: Yes. That's what literature expresses and what the critic has to explain.

CAYLEY: But what does that say to life in the ordinary world, where one encounters good and evil inextricably mixed? How does an imaginative vision get one beyond that?

FRYE: It gets you beyond the relativity of moral judgments. Pascal says there's good on one side of the Pyrenees and evil on the other. Your expressions of what is good and what is bad are usually expressions of an ideology which is concerned with promoting the ascendancy or authority of this as distinct from the ascendancy or authority of that. All good/evil judgments are tentative. You have to try to move, as in the title of one of Nietzsche's books, beyond good and evil.

CAYLEY: He means something rather different, I think.

FRYE: I'm not so sure. He comes to rest finally on a conception of a will to power, which a great many people regard as evil and which in many of its manifestations is.

CAYLEY: Are you saying that good and evil are ultimately unreal?

FRYE: I think the antithesis is unreal. Blake said, "Good is the passive that obeys Reason. Evil is the active springing from Energy." He said that in the context of satire. There is a real hell in Blake, a hell of torture and cruelty and death-wish. But we all live under a structure of authority in which there's a tendency to regard the following of that authority as good and a tendency to regard any effort to break out from it as evil. That is something that always turns out to be inadequate.

CAYLEY: Partly what I'm trying to understand are the political or real-world implications of your thought.

FRYE: The political implications are, again, in the direction of what I've called primary concern. What has thrilled me about the movements in Eastern Europe is that they are not ideological movements. They are movements for fundamental human rights to live and eat and to own property. The authorities there, insofar as they are opposing these demands, are no longer saying, "We are conducting a certain course in the interest of a higher socialist destiny." They are saying, with George Orwell, "The object of power is power, and we're going to hang on to it as long as we've got guns to shoot you with." The protest is made in the direction of something which breaks out of the ideological framework altogether. Some of the protesters are loyal Communists, others would prefer a capitalist system, others are protesting on religious grounds, and so forth. But it's not really an ideological struggle at all. It's a struggle to break clear of the fetters of ideologies.

CAYLEY: In your way of thinking, ideology seems to be the great evil.

FRYE: No, ideology is not evil. It's something essential to human life. The thing is that it has to be subordinate to the very simple and primary things that the imagination is about: life, love, freedom, dignity.

CAYLEY: How can ideology be subordinate to those things?

FRYE: We want to live, but we go to war for ideological reasons. War or terrorism is sold to us as a realistic way of smashing somebody else's ideology.

CAYLEY: Yes, but how would it be possible to invert those relationships, to make primary concern primary and secondary concern secondary? You've said that we can't live without secondary concern, that ideology is not something we can do without.

FRYE: But as long as primary concerns are primary, ideology doesn't have to develop structures of antagonism. It doesn't have to develop structures of enmity.

CAYLEY: I would have thought these things were a part of its nature.

FRYE: Well, they have been a part of its nature, but I think they can be removed from that context. If I adopt, say, an ideological nonconformist position, it doesn't mean I don't respect and love people who have Catholic, Buddhist, Jewish, or other positions. The relativity of ideology to human peace and dignity is what I would insist on. That to me is what the word *liberal* means.

CAYLEY: So you accept the fact that you belong to a place, a tradition, a way of thinking, and that those things for you will inevitably have the aspect of an ideology?

FRYE: Certainly. Oh, yes. I've said over and over again that we belong to something before we are anything. Nine months before I was born I was a middle-class, twentieth-century Canadian intellectual.

CAYLEY: But this can be subordinate to primary concern?

FRYE: The fact that I'm a middle-class Canadian intellectual of the twentieth century doesn't mean that I repudiate what came before the twentieth century, or that I want Canada to assert its ascendancy over something else. I am what I am: let others be what they are.

CAYLEY: To return to this question of politics, you said earlier that one of your reasons for not going to the United States was that you felt an attachment both to the CCF/NDP and to the United Church. You have always been socially engaged and have always reached out. Yet you also say that the historical realm is an arena of illusion. That is, the movement in your thought is toward the permanent structures of human creation and achievement, it's toward the eternal world of the mind, it's away from the illusions of history. So is there really room for political hope, for political action, in your approach?

FRYE: Certainly there is. But the political action, again, has to be action in the light of the vision. Two nations relate to each other. They may be at peace, and they may be at war. But they ought to be at peace, and they have no business going to war.

CAYLEY: So the political is the realm in which vision is enacted.

FRYE: Yes. The longer I've lived the more I realize that I belong in a certain context. Just as a plant grows in the soil, I am in a Canadian context. The more completely I am that, I think the more I am acceptable to others. It's the law in literature, which I've often expressed, of Faulkner's devoting himself to a county with an unpronounceable name in Mississippi and getting the Nobel Prize in Sweden.

CAYLEY: What, in your view, is the path to making primary concern primary? At times you've spoken of the university as the engine-room of society, particularly when someone elso has called it an ivory tower. Is education the pathway?

FRYE: All pathways are educational pathways, yes. If you're going in any direction at all, it has to be some kind of educational direction.

CAYLEY: Then how do you see the university in relation to society?

FRYE: I see the university as standing for the permanent realities of life. The one form of improvement or progress is science. The one form of stability in human life is the arts and the products of the imagination, which, as I say, include religion. The university is the place that safeguards and promotes those.

CAYLEY: How do think the university is doing in that regard?

FRYE: It's struggling with inadequate budgets.

CAYLEY: But that's not all it's struggling with. It's struggling, for example, with a growing specialization, and a growing domination by anti-intellectual ideologies and interest groups. The decline of the university is the theme of a number of currently popular laments. Now I'm sure the decline of the university has been a staple theme since there was a university, but there does seem to be an especially acute sense of crisis at the moment.

FRYE: I think that there is. The university has always had to struggle with the fact that scholarship is specialized on the one hand and the fact that students have to be taught on the other. The problem is to specialize without going into all the hysterias of pedantry, and to teach without going into the vulgarities of popularization.

CAYLEY: And how is that going at the moment?

FRYE: What I know best is the study of literature. I don't think it's impossible for a person to be a specialist in a literary area and at the same time be able to communicate literature to students in a way that doesn't insult their intelligence.

CAYLEY: I understand that, but I guess I'm talking more about the big picture. Take a book like Allan Bloom's *The Closing of the American Mind*. Without mentioning Bloom's name you satirize this book very effectively in one of your recent essays, but I'm not sure whether you're concealing from your readers how much of it you think is true.

FRYE: I thought the student activist movement of the sixties was mistaken in the sense that it was not a movement from genuine social roots, but I don't brood over it. I don't feel it is something in the light of which we have to consider a drastic reform of universities. I distrust all quack remedies, and I distrust all back-to-basics movements, simply because they begin with the phrase "back to." I don't know how I could put that more clearly, really, except to say that there are no quick-fix cures.

CAYLEY: This is also part of not having an argument.

FRYE: That's right.

CAYLEY: To you all educational prescriptions, such as Bloom's, are inevitably ideological. They won't change anything, they'll just establish another equally blind regime, though the blindness might take a different form.

FRYE: They just turn the wheel of history. The word *revolution* has two meanings. One is the upheaval of the social order. The other is turning a wheel. And eventually one meaning of the word *revolution* gives place to the other.

CAYLEY: You seemed to suggest a moment ago that if one didn't go to university, one didn't have much hope of learning to make primary concern primary.

FRYE: I see the university as very central in the educational process, but of course it's only one of many institutions that are concerned to safeguard the permanent values of what I mean by the arts and sciences. If I said that going to university or being attached to the university was a sine qua non, a condition of human freedom and dignity, I would be talking nonsense.

CAYLEY: Why?

FRYE: Because it's so obvious that one can be a fully developed human being without going near a university.

CAYLEY: Could one be a fully developed human being without reading?

FRYE: In our society, it would be very difficult to be a fully developed human being without reading, that's true.

CAYLEY: So you're just saying that one could get an education another way, not that one could be fully developed in your sense without an education.

FRYE: Yes. Any specific program of education, like going to college, is expendable. I once had a student say that he was rather frustrated by having gone through a university course and wound up knowing what his grandmother had always known without ever having heard of a university. There is, I think, a built-in wisdom in the human mind, which is a part of its need to survive. And that can work itself out in almost any social area.

CAYLEY: And yet again and again you emphasize the need for training, for practice, for *habitus*.

FRYE: Yes, everybody needs to have a sense of self-fulfillment, and the self-fulfillment has to be in the direction of acquiring skills and powers which can be acquired only by practice. Aristotle begins his *Metaphysics* by saying that all men by nature desire to know. It's not so much a question of what they know. It's the desire for self-fulfillment.

CAYLEY: Have you ever wondered whether education is wasted on the young?

FRYE: It's like Bernard Shaw says, "Youth is too valuable to be wasted on the young." You're rather stuck with it. I think that students at university have many obstacles thrown in their way by the pedantry and misunderstandings of their teachers and so forth, but those are human conflicts. We all have those.

CAYLEY: I was privileged to have had four years at Harvard between 1962 and 1966, and if I think of the use I could make of those years now when I know what I want to know, and what I did with them then, I find the contrast appalling.

FRYE: Roland Barthes says all reading is really rereading, and similarly all education is really re-education. Anything effective in your education has to be, I think, a product of hindsight.

CAYLEY: I understand that and appreciate it, but I still think my point has some practical application to the structure of universities.

FRYE: Yes, certainly I'd accept that. A lot of students go through university with very little profit, and the fact that they go through with very little profit is not always their fault by any means. I quite agree with that.

CAYLEY: In your scheme of the three phases of language, which in *The Great Code* you borrow from Vico, you suggest along with Vico that at the end there's a *ricorso*, a return. And you say a similar thing in your sequence of modes in the *Anatomy* — that underneath or behind irony, myth begins to reappear. You have been able to take a synoptic view of the history of language, the history of literature, the history of our civilization, to see these histories in a way that makes them all present at once for you. This vast learning seems to be characteristic of our age. We stand at what sometimes seems to be the end of a tradition, encompassing it all. At one time Spengler was important for you. Later on you satirized him and made jokes about The Great Western Butterslide. Did you once accept the idea of decline in Spengler, and do you wonder now what's next?

FRYE: I'm not sure I ever reacted to the word *decline* in Spengler's book. The vision I got from Spengler was not a vision of decline. It was a vision of maturing to a certain point. The question of cycle always turns up. There is a cycle in Vico, it's a little different in Spengler, but it's a cycle again in Toynbee. As I've said often, every cycle is a failed spiral. When you get to the end of the cycle, what should be done is to encompass the entire structure up to that point on another level, not just to go back to the beginning, although there's going to be a certain amount of that.

CAYLEY: Do you see instances in history of spiralling rather than cycling?

FRYE: We find the idea of the turning cycle in the movement that went from the decline and fall of the Roman Empire to the medieval civilization. People always thought in terms of a renewed Roman Empire, all the way down to the eighteenth century, and they certainly regarded that as a spiral. Whether we would think so or not is another question.

CAYLEY: I would think there's some argument for it. So the question then becomes whether we take our tradition with us on another turn, or whether, as appears to be the case and was noted in your remarks on senility earlier, we forget it.

FRYE: I think it's a disaster to forget it, because that means that anything new will simply be the primitive coming around again, making the same mistakes all over. And we can't afford to make those mistakes with the technology we've got now.

CAYLEY: And yet a tradition can also be a burden.

FRYE: It's hard, yes.

CAYLEY: One feels that your ability to sum up an entire tradition is something that can't continue.

FRYE: It seems to me that that is part of what the word *university* means. It's a matter of the universe, the "one turning," a matter of wrapping things up in a single form. You have to start at a center. It takes a long time to get to any kind of intelligible circumference. But if you keep on going you can eventually get there.

NOTES

1. John Ayre, *Northrop Frye: A Biography*, Random House, Toronto, 1989, p. 4
2. See p. 113
3. Frye, *Anatomy of Criticism*, Princeton University Press, 1957, p. 142
4. William Blake, *A Descriptive Catalogue*, in *The Complete Poetry and Prose of William Blake*, ed. David Erdman, University of California Press, Berkeley, 1982, p. 542 (All subsequent Blake citations are from this volume.)
5. *Anatomy of Criticism*, p. 122
6. *Anatomy of Criticism*, p. 122n
7. Ayre, pp. 54–55
8. John and Elizabeth Newson, "Cultural Aspects of Child-rearing in the English-speaking World," in *The Integration of the Child into the Social World*, ed. Martin Richards, Cambridge University Press, 1974, p. 56
9. Ayre, p. 44
10. Ayre, p. 45
11. Ayre, p. 45
12. Blake, *The Everlasting Gospel*, p. 521
13. Blake, *Annotations to Swedenborg's Divine Love and Divine Wisdom*, p. 603
14. Frye, *Fearful Symmetry*, Princeton University Press, 1947, p. 32
15. *Fearful Symmetry*, p. 31

16. *Ideas*, CBC Radio, Oct. 14, 1991

17. Frye, *The Double Vision: Language and Meaning in Religion*, United Church Publishing House, 1991, p. 11

18. Blake, *There Is No Natural Religion*, p. 2

19. Ayre, p. 116

20. See p. 61

21. *Fearful Symmetry*, p. 13

22. *The Double Vision*, pp. 47–48

23. See p. 89

24. See p. 92

25. *The Ideas of Northrop Frye*, *Ideas*, CBC Radio, Feb. 19, 1990, p. 3

26. Frye, *Divisions on a Ground: Essays on Canadian Culture*, Anansi, Toronto, 1982, p. 99

27. See A. C. Hamilton, *Northrop Frye: An Anatomy of His Criticism*, University of Toronto Press, 1990, pp. 207–208 for further discussion of this point.

28. C. S. Lewis, *Surprised By Joy*, Harcourt, Brace and World, New York, 1955, p. 167

29. Frye, *The Stubborn Structure*, Cornell University Press, Ithaca, New York, 1970, p. 173

30. *The Double Vision*, p. 32

31. *The Double Vision*, p. 35

32. Hamilton, p. xiv

33. *The Ideas of Northrop Frye*, p. 14

34. Hamilton, p. 207

35. Frye, *Myth and Metaphor: Selected Essays 1974–1988*, University of Virginia Press, Charlottesville, Virginia, 1990, p. 162

36. *The Double Vision*, p. 39

37. See Frye's discussion of Emily Dickinson in *Fables of Identity: Studies in Poetic Mythology*, Harcourt, Brace and World, New York, 1963

38. Frye, *The Critical Path: An Essay on the Social Context of Literary Criticism*, Indiana University Press, Bloomington, Indiana, 1971, p. 97

39. *Myth and Metaphor*, p. 197

40. Frye, *Creation and Recreation*, University of Toronto Press, 1980, p. 28

41. Ayre, p. 111

42. Frye, *Spiritus Mundi: Essays on Literature, Myth and Society*, Indiana University Press, Bloomington, Indiana, 1976, p. 15

43. Ayre, p. 114

44. Blake, *Annotations to Thornton*, p. 669

45. Blake, *The Book of Urizen*, pp. 70–83

46. Blake, p. 560

47. Frye, *A Study of English Romanticism*, Random House, New York, 1968, p. 15

48. See Owen Barfield, *The Rediscovery of Meaning and Other Essays*, Wesleyan University Press, Middleton, Conn., 1977

49. Imre Salusinszky, *Criticism in Society*, Methuen, New York, 1987, p. 62

50. *Anatomy of Criticism*, p. vii
51. *Anatomy of Criticism*, p. 16
52. Frye, *The Secular Scripture: A Study of the Structure of Romance*, Harvard University Press, Cambridge, Mass., 1976, pp. 60–61
53. Reaney's remark was made in an unpublished interview with the author.
54. Frye, *The Educated Imagination*, CBC Publication, 1963
55. *Anatomy of Criticism*, p. 13
56. *Anatomy of Criticism*, p. 8
57. *Anatomy of Criticism*, p. 45
58. *Anatomy of Criticism*, p. 8
59. *Anatomy of Criticism*, p. 15
60. *Anatomy of Criticism*, p. 17
61. *Anatomy of Criticism*, p. 4
62. Frye wrote this before Thomas Kuhn introduced the idea that the history of science is marked by a series of incommensurable paradigms rather than a linear progression.
63. Frye, *The Great Code: The Bible and Literature*, Harcourt Brace Jovanovich, New York, 1982, p. 50
64. T. S. Eliot, *Four Quartets*, Harcourt, Brace and World, New York, 1943, p. 3
65. *The Educated Imagination*, p. 44
66. Hamilton, p. 17
67. *Anatomy of Criticism*, p. 349
68. Blake, p. 560
69. *The Secular Scripture*, p. 36
70. Hamilton, p. 32
71. *Anatomy of Criticism*, p. 97
72. *Northrop Frye in Modern Criticism*, ed. Murray Krieger, Columbia University Press, New York, 1966, p. 1
73. Irving Layton, "The Excessively Quiet Groves," in *Cerberus: Poems by Louis Dudek, Irving Layton and Raymond Souster*, Contact Press, Toronto, 1952, p. 55
74. *Delta* 5, Oct. 1958, pp. 26–27
75. *Toronto*, Oct. 1986, p. 8
76. *Psychoanalysis and Literary Process*, ed. Frederick Crews, Winthrop, Cambridge, Mass., 1970, pp. 1–24
77. Frederic Jameson, *The Political Unconscious: Narrative as a Socially Symbolic Act*, Cornell University Press, Ithaca, New York, 1981, pp. 68–75
78. *Myth and Metaphor*, p. 93
79. Donald R. Riccomini, "Northrop Frye and Structuralism: Identity and Difference," *University of Toronto Quarterly* 49, Fall 1979, pp. 33–47
80. "Structure, Sign and Play in the Discourse of the Human Sciences," in *The Structuralist Controversy*, Johns Hopkins University Press, Baltimore, 1970

81. Eliot, p. 5
82. *Nostalgia for the Absolute* was the title of Steiner's 1974 Massey Lectures for CBC Radio (CBC Publications).
83. *Creation and Recreation*, p. 72
84. *Anatomy of Criticism*, p. 4
85. *Myth and Metaphor*, pp. 235–236
86. "There Is Really No Such Thing as Methodology," *Orbit* 11, Feb. 1970, p. 5
87. *The Stubborn Structure*, p. 171
88. *Spiritus Mundi*, p. 106
89. *Myth and Metaphor*, p. 81
90. Blake, *The Laocoön*, p. 274
91. *Spiritus Mundi*, p. 107
92. "The spirit is taken over by a mythical and metaphorical organism, with its historical roots in the Bible, and the integrity of that organism is his Muse, the mother that brings to life a being separate both from herself and from him." (*Spiritus Mundi*, p. 18)
93. *The Great Code*, p. 18
94. *Myth and Metaphor*, p. 122
95. Blake, *All Religions Are One*, p. 1
96. *Myth and Metaphor*, p. 98
97. *The Great Code*, p. 227. See also the final pages of *Creation and Recreation*.
98. *Myth and Metaphor*, p. 98
99. *Myth and Metaphor*, p. 104
100. Blake, *There Is No Natural Religion*, p. 2
101. *Globe and Mail*, Feb. 27, 1982, p. E7
102. William O. Fennell, "Theology and Frye: Some Implications of *The Great Code*," *Toronto Journal of Theology* I/1, 1985, pp. 113–121
103. *Myth and Metaphor*, p. 42
104. Donald Wiebe, "The 'Centripetal Theology' of *The Great Code*," *Toronto Journal of Theology* I/1, 1985, pp. 122–127
105. *Myth and Metaphor*, p. 42
106. *The Secular Scripture*, p. 92
107. *Anatomy of Criticism*, p. 308
108. Vaclav Havel, "Stories and Totalitarianism," *The Idler* 18, July/Aug. 1988, pp. 8–19
109. See Chapter Six of *The Educated Imagination*
110. *Myth and Metaphor*, p. 103
111. See p. 111
112. See p. 15
113. *The Double Vision*, p. 50
114. Ayre, p. 25
115. Ayre, p. 44
116. This refers to the hymn "Lead Kindly Light" with words by John Henry Newman (#270 in *The Hymn Book of The United Church of Canada and the Anglican Church of Canada*, 1971).

117. "Structure, Sign and Play in the Discourse of the Human Sciences," p. 249

118. Thomas J. J. Altizer, *The New Apocalypse: The Radical Christian Vision of William Blake*, Michigan State University Press, 1967

119. Unpublished interview. Kathleen Raine is a British poet and scholar and the author of a number of books on Blake, including *Blake and Tradition* (Princeton University Press, 1968), *The Human Face of God* (Thames and Hudson, London, 1982), and *Blake and the New Age* (Allen and Unwin, London, 1979).

120. Blake, *A Descriptive Catalogue*, pp. 541–542

121. *William Blake: Prophet of a New Age, Ideas*, CBC Radio, March 26, 1987, p. 20

122. *Spiritus Mundi*, p. 15

123. *The Stubborn Structure*, p. 174

124. Blake, *Jerusalem*, p. 153

125. Thomas Rymer, *Short View of Tragedy*, 1692

126. Samuel Johnson, *Prologue to the Opening of Drury Lane Theatre*, 1747

127. See n. 76

128. See n. 77

129. "Ghostlier Demarcations," in *Northrop Frye in Modern Criticism*, pp. 68–75

130. Blake, *The Marriage of Heaven and Hell*, p. 35

131. Sir Thomas Browne, "All Things are artificial, for nature is the art of God," in *Religio Medici*, Part 1, section 15, 1643

132. *The Critical Path*, pp. 59–64

133. "The Drunken Boat: The Revolutionary Element in Romanticism, in *The Stubborn Structure*, pp. 200–217

134. Frye, *Fables of Identity*, Harcourt Brace, New York, 1963, pp. 238–255

135. Interview by Stan Correy and Don Anderson, in *A World in a Grain of Sand: Twenty-Two Interviews with Northrop Frye*, ed. Robert D. Denham, Peter Lang, New York, 1991, pp. 221–235

136. Ayre, p. 180

137. Harold Adams Innis and Marshall McLuhan were both colleagues of Frye's at the University of Toronto. See Innis, *The Bias of Communications*, University of Toronto Press, 1951, and McLuhan, *Understanding Media*, McGraw Hill, New York, 1964.

138. Historian Donald G. Creighton was another of Frye's University of Toronto colleagues. See Creighton, *The Commercial Empire of the St. Lawrence*, Ryerson Press, Toronto, 1937.

139. These annual reviews are collected in *The Bush Garden*, Anansi, Toronto, 1971.

140. Eric Havelock was a colleague of Frye's at the University of Toronto in the 1940s. In 1977, the year before he died, he returned to U of T to address a symposium on orality and literacy, held at Emmanuel College. His views are summarized in his final book, *The Muse Learns to Write*, Yale University Press, New Haven, Conn., 1986.

141. The Macpherson Commission was named for its chairman, the dis-

tinguished political philosopher C. B. Macpherson. It was established in response to student criticism of the University of Toronto's undergraduate curriculum, with its scholarly and specialized honors courses. The commission reported in 1967 and recommended that the university virtually eliminate these courses, offer the students more choice, but still maintain high academic standards. (See *C. B. Macpherson: A Retrospective*, *Ideas*, May 24, 1988, p. 12)

142. Claude Bissell was the president of the University of Toronto at the time of the Macpherson Commission.
143. Blake, *The Laocoön*, pp. 273–275
144. *The Letter to the Hebrews*, Chapter 11
145. See n. 102
146. See for example Bill Devall and George Sessions, *Deep Ecology*, Peregrine Smith Books, Salt Lake City, 1985